Sharing Jesus

REPRODUCIBLE EVANGELISM TRAINING MANUAL

COMMUNICATING CHRIST EFFECTIVELY

DOUGLAS SHAW

Gospel Light is an evangelical Christian publisher dedicated to serving the local church. We believe God's vision for Gospel Light is to provide church leaders with biblical, user-friendly materials that will help them evangelize, disciple and minister to children, youth and families.

We hope this Gospel Light resource will help you discover biblical truth for your own life and help you minister to adults. God bless you in your work.

For a free catalog of resources from Gospel Light please contact your Christian supplier or contact us at 1-800-4-GOSPEL or at www.gospellight.com.

PUBLISHING STAFF
William T. Greig, Publisher
Dr. Elmer L. Towns, Senior Consulting Publisher
Dr. Gary S. Greig, Senior Consulting Editor
Jill Honodel, Editor
Pam Weston, Assistant Editor
Patti Virtue, Editorial Assistant
Kyle Duncan, Associate Publisher
Bayard Taylor, M.Div., Senior Editor, Theological and Biblical Issues
Barbara LeVan Fisher, Cover Designer
Debi Thayer, Designer

ISBN 0-8307-2142-8

Printed in U.S.A.

How to Make Clean Copies from This Book

You may make copies of portions of this book with a clean conscience if:

- you (or someone in your organization) are the original purchaser;
- you are using the copies you make for a noncommercial purpose (such as teaching or promoting your ministry) within your church or organization;
- you follow the instructions provided in this book.

However, it is ILLEGAL for you to make copies if:

- you are using the material to promote, advertise or sell a product or service other than for ministry fund-raising;
- you are using the material in or on a product for sale;
- you or your organization are **not** the original purchaser of this book.

By following these guidelines you help us keep our products affordable.
Thank you,
Gospel Light

Contents

Foreword

Despite the pluralism in society, the thirst for salvation through Christ is still a driving force in people's lives. Lost and wandering souls seek salvation through self-help, self-service cults, New Age philosophies and other religious experiences.

Sharing Jesus is an invaluable resource to present the gospel of Jesus Christ in a pluralistic world. You will be equipped not only with the power of Jesus Christ and His purpose to save mankind, but also the practical understanding of the strategies of the enemy, what makes Jesus unique and how to overcome the odds, turn the tables and take back what is rightfully God's.

There are many who will not read Christian literature, tune in to Christian radio or television or attend a gathering at a Christian church. But they will be open to talking to a Christian friend or neighbor who is willing to share the truth in love. The task of spreading the gospel of God's love is the responsibility of every Christian. This is a course for the whole church to use in learning to reach out to the lost.

Sharing Jesus is a necessary tool for our calling to be lights in a dark world.

—Reverend Reinhard Bonnke

Introduction

The Changeless Gospel in a Changing World

The gospel of the Lord Jesus Christ is both *timeless* and *triumphant.* Over the centuries, devilish forces have tried to conquer it and earthly rulers have tried to crush it. Skeptics have suspected it, atheists avoided it and cultists corrupted it. But the *truth* marches on and abides forever.

The world around us is in *transition.* It is constantly changing. The dramatic de-Christianizing attempts in the western world, particularly since the 1970s, demand new approaches to the spiritually lost. Seekers are asking questions that much of the Church is not answering and they are receiving answers for questions that are irrelevant to their search.

The definition of spiritual meaning has evolved into something very different from what it was even two decades ago. Outside the Church doors are whirlwinds of tolerance, multiculturalism and globalism. Inside the Church doors, we struggle with reshuffled priorities that have shifted focus from the spiritually lost and downplayed the importance of personal witnessing. Meanwhile, the *task* to fulfill the Great Commission remains unchanged. It is a mandate that has never been withdrawn by the Lord of the harvest.

The primary focus of this study course is not intended to be erudite scholarship, exhaustive apologetics or just another elective study course. It is intended to present an *action plan.* It is an action plan aimed at the target audience of somewhere between 120 and 150 million—a group that has been neglected while the Church has been busy with lesser priorities, sustaining heavy losses. It is an action plan which is biblically accurate and Christcentered. But above all, it is a way of life that can turn our world around, as we win the lost one by one through the power of the love and truth of the gospel, before it is too late.

My fascination with one-on-one personal witnessing began with my yogi grandfather who, following a fruitless six-year search in India's Himalayas, found Christ after reading the Gospel of John. My desire for personal witnessing then gained momentum when I got involved in outdoor evangelism for the express purpose of planting churches in a hostile environment. Its growth further accelerated when I became a minister of evangelism at a church in northern California. My desire now is to ignite a passion for personal evangelism in you.

At a time when many Christians have abandoned dialogue with non-Christians and settled for living in the comfort zone surrounded by other Christians, personal evangelism has become a matter that demands our highest attention. No particular "method" is sacred, only the *truth* is. However, the fact is that with the right approach, God-given results follow and personal witnessing becomes excitingly self-perpetuating!

The ripened harvest fields of the world and the Lord of the harvest continue to wait for the messenger. How long will you keep them waiting?

—Douglas Shaw

The Purpose

To educate, encourage and empower any Christian to share in understanding and love a personal witness with unbelievers, leading them to Jesus Christ as Savior and Lord. It is intended to purposefully stimulate, not just defenders of the faith, but also sharers of the faith who will present a relevant gospel in a changing world.

Who Can Use the Study

Pastors, lay leaders and any Christian who wants to learn to witness one-on-one with confidence, or to sharpen present evangelistic skills.

This course is best used in a small group study for a Sunday or weekday class. It can also be used for personal study or even adapted for a series of Sunday morning messages. It has the flexibility to be utilized for six to twelve sessions.

The Plan

This valuable study has been designed to fit a variety of learning situations:

- You have a choice of course lengths—from 6 to 12 sessions.
- You have a choice of session lengths—from 60 to 90 minutes.
- You have a choice of settings—in a classroom or home Bible study.
- You have a choice of meeting time (Sunday or weekday mornings, Sunday or weekday evenings or a concentrated seminar or retreat) and frequency (once a week, every day or evening for a week, or a weekend retreat).

This leader's guide is a useful resource, offering stimulating and enjoyable opportunities for group study to lead Christians into becoming personal witnesses for God. It is unique because it...

- Offers the flexibility of completing the study in 6 to 12 sessions.
- Contains all the necessary resources, including reproducible student pages and leader's instructions, in one easy-to-use book.
- Is filled with valuable information and motivation to become personal witnesses of the gospel of Jesus Christ.
- Includes interactive lessons to enable students to learn from the experiences and insights of others.
- Requires very few additional supplies for class sessions. An overhead projector, white board or chalkboard are helpful, but not necessary. Suggested supplies and preparations of materials are listed at the beginning of each session.
- Suggests practical actions for participants to take in implementing each session's learning.

How to Use This Study

Each session contains the following components:

Introduction introduces the session to the leader and may be used as a 30-second introduction to the session.

Objective states the purpose of the session.

Key Verse presents the Scripture focus of the session.

Preparation is divided into three sections:

- **Pray** gives suggested prayer focus for the leader.
- **Prepare** gives practical steps for leaders to prepare for the lessons.
- **Practice** encourages the leader to participate with students in the Take Action steps.

Lesson Plan provides the leader with the directions and information needed to lead the study.

Reproducible Student Handouts provides the student materials needed for the lesson.

The Lesson Plan

Each session has several different active learning activities to guide the students through the topic. Each lesson contains activities that teach the main focus as well as optional activities to extend the topic for two sessions. The activities labeled as **Step 1**, **Step 2**, etc. are those that teach the main focus of the session. The supplementary activities are labeled **Option**.

A suggested amount of time is found at the beginning of each activity to aid the leader in planning the session. If you are teaching each session in only one hour, use the two or three essential activities first, then as time permits add optional activities.

Optional activities are set apart in a box to alert the leader. These options explore aspects of each main point that could not be addressed in the shorter time schedules. These can be used to extend the session over two meetings or enhance the lesson at the leader's discretion.

Each session is divided into part A and part B by the following stop sign and instruction:

Two-Meeting Track: If you want to spread the session over two meetings, stop here and close in prayer. Inform students of the content to be covered in your next meeting.

Meanings of Symbols

✞ PRAY
❏ PREPARATION
➻ LEADER'S DIRECTION
💡 OPTIONAL ACTIVITY
☛ SUGGESTION

The following elements will be found at the *end* of each session:

- TAKE ACTION is a take-home resource that contains practical applications to challenge students to apply the lesson to their lives.
- ILLUSTRATION contains a story and discussion or application questions that are related to the session topic. It can be used in class as an optional activity, or as another take-home resource to aid students in applying the lesson.
- REPRODUCIBLE PAGES to be photocopied for students to use during activities.

A Final Suggestion

It is strongly recommended that group members bring a notebook/folder to each session for taking notes and for keeping the handouts together.

Session 1

The Message

Jesus—His Person, His Power and His Purpose

Introduction

Since the dawn of civilization, atheists and agnostics have spent an inordinate amount of time questioning the existence and relevancy of God. Even after the personal appearance of Jesus Christ—God in human flesh—onto the landscape of human history, there have been ongoing attempts to dilute, dismiss and even destroy His gospel of hope for all people on our planet.

The divinely dramatic significance is clear: Jesus Christ walked into time and quietly divided it into B.C. and A.D. He walked into our perceptions of who God is and we are now redeemed or rejected on the basis of whether or not we are filled with His truth and His Spirit. His question to the apostle Peter echoes through the corridors of time and eternity: "Who do [people] say that I, the Son of Man, am?" (Matthew 16:13). Jesus Christ is the central issue that needs a response from the seeking heart.

Objective

In this session we will explore the biblical Jesus Christ—His person is unique, His power unparalleled and His purpose universal. We will also discover how He lovingly intends to reach all of His creation with the touch of His divine transformation.

Key Verses

"In the beginning was the Word, and the Word was with God, and the Word was God. He was in the beginning with God. All things were made through Him, and without Him nothing was made that was made. In Him was life, and the life was the light of men. And the light shines in the darkness, and the darkness did not comprehend it." John 1:1-5

Preparation

Pray

- ✞ Ask God to speak to you in a fresh new way through His Word and Spirit concerning the uniqueness of Jesus Christ.
- ✞ Ask God to prepare the hearts of those you will lead in this study, so that they will realize afresh the uniqueness of who Jesus is, what He has done in their lives and what more He desires to do.
- ✞ Ask God for results—fruit from this learning experience that will be evident to group members as they actually start sharing the faith.

Prepare

- ❑ Read through the material thoroughly.
- ❑ Based on your personal reflection and the knowledge of who will attend the class, anticipate questions that they might ask and how you might answer them scripturally.
- ❑ Think through all items in this session—questions for consideration or discussion to help you guide the class in the right direction and avoid sidetracks and fruitless discussion.
- ❑ For Session 1A: Photocopy student handouts "Distinctives: Who Is This Jesus Christ?" (p. 21); "His Roots, His Roles and His Redemption" (p. 22). **Option:** Make an overhead transparency of "Desire: The Motivation of Jesus Christ Was Love" or make photocopies, one for each group member (p. 23).
- ❑ For Session 1B: "Dynamic: The Mighty Power in Jesus Christ" (pp. 24-25); **Option:** Photocopy "Illustration: The Testimony of Ishwar Dayal" (p. 26) for each group member.
- ❑ Provide Bibles, paper, pens or pencils for those who might need them.
- ❑ Photocopy "The Message: Jesus—His Person, His Power and His Purpose: Take Action" sheet (pp. 19-20) for each group member.

Practice

At the end of each session is a Take Action plan. Use it to summarize the session, go over the action plan with students and encourage them to follow through on the action plan. As the leader of the study, you are strongly encouraged to practice what is learned so that you can share from your experiences—both the successes and failures—to help stimulate discussion and edify the class, as well as set an example for them to follow.

Session 1A

Introduce the Session (10 Minutes)

✞ Begin the session by praying that God's presence, power and uniqueness would be made evident and that everyone would have eyes to see and ears to hear the truth about who the person of Jesus Christ is.

➻ Welcome the class members and have everyone introduce themselves and *briefly* describe how they first heard about Jesus Christ.

Step 1: Distinctives: Who Is This Jesus Christ? (20 Minutes)

➻ Hand out copies of "Distinctives: Who Is This Jesus Christ?" and pens or pencils.

➻ Divide the class into groups of four or five, assigning a leader to each group.

➻ Give students five minutes to individually complete their handouts, then discuss their responses in their small groups. Instruct the groups to work together to add Scripture to support their positions.

➻ Have small groups share their scriptural support for their points of view with the whole group.

Step 2: His Roots, His Roles and His Redemption (20 Minutes)

➻ Give each student a copy of "His Roots, His Roles and His Redemption."

➻ Have students remain in (or return to) their small groups.

➻ Instruct students to look up the scriptural references and discuss the descriptions.

The answers for the student handout are in parentheses:

Roots: Where Did He Come From?

1. Revelation 1:8 (Alpha and Omega, the Beginning and the End)
2. John 1:14 (God's only Son)
3. Mark 1:24; John 6:69 (The Messiah without sin)
4. Colossians 1:15 (Jesus' rule over all creation)

Roles: Who Is He?

5. Revelation 19:16 (King of kings and Lord of lords)
6. John 1:41; 4:25,26 (Christ, the anointed One)
7. Colossians 1:15; 2:9 (The invisible God in bodily form)
8. John 6:32,33,35 (The Bread of Life)

Redemption: What Did He Come to Provide for Humanity?

9. John 11:23-26; 1 Corinthians 15:55-57 (Victory over death through His resurrection)
10. Luke 1:47; 2:11 (Salvation)

11. John 1:29,36 (Atonement for sin)
12. John 14:1-3 (The promise of heaven)

➻ Discuss "A Point to Ponder and Discuss" with the whole group.

Option: Desire: The Motivation of Jesus Christ Was Love (15 Minutes)

➻ Give each student a copy of "Desire: The Motivation of Jesus Christ Was Love" and a pen or pencil. Or make a transparency of the student handout to display on an overhead projector.

Introduce the lesson by asking volunteers to read the verses. Explain the following history of humanity's relationship with God, then discuss the questions with the whole group.

Humanity's Relationship to God

- Creation: He made us (see Genesis 1:1,26,27).
- Crisis: In our sinful state, we needed Him to redeem us (see Romans 5:8).
- Calling: He called us to glorify Him, both now and eternally (see Romans 8:28-30).

☛ **Suggestion:** Have the group members return to their small groups to discuss #5.

Two-Meeting Track: If you want to spread the session over two meetings, stop here and close in prayer. Inform students of the content to be covered in your next meeting.

Session 1B

Preparation

Pray

- ✞ Ask God to refresh your memory as to how He led you to Himself in His own unique way and praise Him for it.
- ✞ Ask God to illuminate those you will lead in this session so that they will grasp the unique way in which He lead them to Himself.
- ✞ Ask God to lead group members as they share the gospel with the lost.

Prepare

- ❑ Photocopy student handouts "Dynamic: The Mighty Power in Jesus Christ" (pp. 24-25 and "Illustration: The Testimony of Ishwar Dayal" (p. 26).

Introduce the Session (10 Minutes)

- ✞ Begin the session by praying that group members will understand the unique expression of God's love and how to apply His uniqueness in their personal testimonies.
- ➻ Welcome students and explain: **Last time we discussed who Jesus is and why He came to earth.**
- ➻ Ask volunteers to share where Jesus came from, who He is and why He came to earth.

Option: Design: How Does God's Love Plan Work Through Jesus Christ? (15 Minutes)

Introduce the lesson by explaining: **God had a plan for expressing His love through Jesus Christ. It was not an afterthought but a detailed plan involving all of history and all humanity.**

- ➻ Assign class members to read the following Scripture references aloud, then discuss the expressions of God's love described in each of the references.

  - **Advanced Planning:** Revelation 13:8: "The Lamb [was] slain from the foundation of the world."
  - **Atonement:** 1 John 2:2: "He is the atoning sacrifice for our sins" (*NIV*).
  - **All People:** Acts 2:21: "Whoever calls on the name of the Lord, shall be saved."

➻ Assign the following Scripture references to different group members to be read aloud before each Scripture is discussed. Then explain, **To clearly understand the pre-Christian spiritual condition Jesus came to redeem, let's discuss the meaning of the following passages** (answers appear in parentheses):

- Ephesians 2:1-3 (We were dead in our trespasses and sins.)
- Ephesians 5:1-8 (We were in darkness.)
- Romans 6:15-18 (We were slaves to sin.)
- John 3:18 (We were condemned already.)
- Isaiah 64:6 (All our righteousness was as filthy rags.)
- Galatians 4:3-5 (Jesus Christ came in the "fullness of time.")

➻ Make the following observations:
Some examples of how Jesus Christ came in the "fullness of time":

1. **The Roman Empire provided a stable government and good roads which allowed for swifter movement of the gospel.**
2. **The Jews suffered under the oppression of the Roman rule. Their misery made them eager for the coming of the promised Messiah.**
3. **The Greeks provided a common language.**

➻ Discuss:
These circumstances were divinely designed, not just coincidental. What specific circumstances in your own life were divinely designed so that you could be in full relationship with Jesus Christ?

Step 3: Dynamic: The Mighty Power in Jesus Christ (30 Minutes)

➻ Give each class member a copy of the handout "Dynamic: The Mighty Power in Jesus Christ."

➻ If you have not already done so, divide group into small groups of four or five.
Introduce the activity: **Aside from personal subjective experiences, there are objective historical and biblical facts that establish the uniqueness of the Lord Jesus Christ. He was and is unlike any other religious or spiritual leader.**

➻ Have the small groups complete the handout together, matching the verses with the correct descriptions.

➻ Answers for the activities are as follows:

His *Life* Was Unprecedented

1. Matthew 1:23
2. 2 Corinthians 5:21
3. Matthew 20:28
4. Matthew 28:5-7
5. Matthew 25:31-34
6. John 14:6
7. Matthew 28:18-20

His *Teaching* Was Unparalleled

8. John 8:28,29
9. Luke 24:25-27
10. Matthew 10:29-31
11. Hebrews 1:1-3
12. John 14:8,9
13. Luke 19:10
14. John 8:9-11
15. Matthew 11:29,30
16. Ephesians 2:8
17. John 10:4,27
18. John 5:24; 6:44; 14:2
19. Acts 26:18

His Long-Term *Influence* Is Unmatched

➻ Read and discuss the remaining section of the handout with the whole group, sharing the following information of how the gospel has spread and will continue to spread throughout the world:

- Witness to His gospel *commenced* with the disciples such as Thomas who was known as the doubter (see John 20:24-29). **After having personally seen and touched the risen Christ, he took the message of His salvation to India. The Church he planted in the first century is now a growing spiritual force penetrating the spiritual darkness. The fellow disciples travelled to other parts of the world to fulfill the Great Commission.**
- Witness to the gospel *continues* with missionaries such as William Carey (1761-1834) who is known as the father of modern missions. **Not only did he, a former cobbler, translate the Bible into 25 languages of India, but he published grammars in four languages and catalogued the flora of India. He was also a leading figure in the abolition of the cultural practice of *suttee*, or widow burning.**

  The continent of Africa has seen the darkness pierced by the pioneering spirit of missionaries such as Mar Slessor and David Livingston. In China the seeds of the gospel were sown by missionaries such as Eric Lidell (featured in *Chariots of Fire*), Hudson Taylor and C. T. Studd.

History records the missions achievements of others as well: Jim Elliott who died a martyr at the hands of the Auca Indians, Raymond Lull of Oxford University who was one of the first missionaries to the Muslims, and Adoniram Judson who served in Burma. Today, the harvest of souls is abundant and worldwide because of these and many other unsung heroes of the faith who sowed unreservedly from their lives, love and labor for the Lord of the harvest, Jesus Christ.

- Witness to the world will be *completed* before the end of time as we know it. Jesus confirmed that fact when He declared that the gospel will be preached to all nations and then shall the end come (see Matthew 24:14). **Every Christian is called to be a witness, to be the light and the salt in this world (see Matthew 5:13-16). Because we have neither control over nor knowledge of God's time clock, there must be a sense of urgency to share the message of salvation, giving every human being we know a chance to escape hell and live in heaven as God intended by accepting the love of the Lord Jesus Christ.**

➻ Return to small groups and have them discuss questions in the "Personal Testimony" section.

Option: Illustration: The Testimony of Ishwar Dayal (10-20 Minutes)

➻ Give each group member a copy of "Illustration: The Testimony of Ishwar Dayal." Ask the group to follow along as you read the story.

➻ After reading the story, ask everyone to briefly outline their testimonies.

➻ Instruct group members to pair up and share their testimonies.

➻ Challenge each one to share his or her testimony with at least one non-Christian during the week.

✞ Close in prayer, asking the Lord to give each of them an opportunity to share his or her testimony.

➻ Ask group members to keep their written testimonies with them for each session. Tell them that you will ask for volunteers to share their testimonies at every class session.

Take Action

➻ Give each member a copy of the Take Action page. Discuss with the whole group. Encourage them to take the actions suggested.

Jesus—His Person, His Power and His Purpose

Take Action

Session Summary

A witnessing Christian must understand and experience the Jesus Christ of the Bible. As we have seen, these *distinctives* include a knowledge of the *roots*, *role* and *redemption* of Jesus Christ. His *desire* to come to earth in human form was motivated by agape love. From the beginning God *designed* a love invasion of humanity in need. The *dynamic* of His life was unprecedented, His teachings unparalleled and His long-term influence unmatched. Ultimately, every human being is faced with a choice to accept or reject Him. Whatever the *decision*, every human being will some day come face to face with Him as Savior or Judge. Power in personal witness is predicated on commitment to His lordship.

Action Plan for the Week

1. Memorize John 1:1-5 by writing it on a 3x5-inch card and putting it in a prominent place where you will see it frequently (i.e., bathroom mirror, refrigerator, computer, etc.).

2. Write out your personal testimony. Remember to include:

    - A description of your religious upbringing;
    - Particular aspects of your pre-Christian life that might be of human interest—your lifestyle, emotions, struggles, etc.;
    - How you saw God working in your life before you became a Christian;
    - Factors that led up to your acceptance of Jesus Christ as Savior and Lord;
    - How you actually accepted Jesus Christ—where, when, how, etc.

3. Share your testimony with at least one non-Christian this week. Make it your prayerful goal to lead that person to seriously consider the uniqueness of the Lord Jesus Christ.

Closing Prayer

Father in heaven, please keep me open to understanding more about who Jesus is every day I live. With the help of your Holy Spirit help me to both experience and express the person, power and purpose of the Lord Jesus Christ. May your truth and Spirit working through me be a witness and light to those around me in spiritual darkness, leading them to accept Jesus Christ as Savior and Lord. In Jesus' name, I pray. Amen.

Distinctives: Who Is This Jesus Christ?

1. Write "Agree" or "Disagree" beside each of the following statements. Then, using Scripture, explain why you agree or disagree.

_____________ a. Jesus Christ is like any other human being.

_____________ b. Jesus Christ is a totally divine being.

_____________ c. Jesus Christ is one of several spiritual masters who represents the true God.

_____________ d. Jesus Christ is a mythological personality, similar to those in Greek and Hindu mythologies.

_____________ e. Jesus Christ is the most respected leader of humanity and the chief seeker of truth.

_____________ f. Jesus Christ is the most profound spiritual and religious symbol in history.

2. Briefly summarize, in your own words, who you think Jesus Christ is.

His Roots, His Roles and His Redemption

Look up the following scriptures and briefly explain the descriptions of Jesus Christ:

Roots: Where Did He Come From?

1. Revelation 1:8

2. John 1:14

3. Mark 1:24; John 6:69

4. Colossians 1:15

Roles: Who Is He?

5. Revelation 19:16

6. John 1:41; 4:25,26

7. Colossians 1:15; 2:9

8. John 6:35,38

Redemption: What Did He Come to Provide for Humanity?

9. John 11:23-26; 1 Corinthians 15:55-57

10. Luke 1:47; 2:11

11. John 1:29,36

12. John 14:1-3

A Point to Ponder and Discuss

How does a Christian's view of Jesus Christ affect his or her ability to share the gospel with others?

Desire: The Motivation of Jesus Christ Was Love

Humanity's Relationship to God

- Creation: He made us (see Genesis 1:1,26,27).
- Crisis: In our sinful state, we needed Him to redeem us (see Romans 5:8).
- Calling: He called us to glorify Him, both now and eternally (see Romans 8:28-30).

1. Read John 3:16 and discuss the following:

   What action did God take?

   What was the motivation behind the action?

   What is the suggested human response to God and the resulting blessing?

2. Complete the following verses from memory, if possible, concerning what God's love is:
   Unconditional:
   Romans 5:8: "God demonstrates His own love toward us, in that while we were still sinners…
   Intentional:
   John 3:16: "God so loved the world that He…
   Relational:
   Revelation 3:20: "Behold, I stand at the door…

3. Read Romans 8:35-39. List the things that cannot separate us from the love of God.

4. If in fact nothing can separate us from the love of God, why then do we at times feel separated from His love?

5. Share briefly with your group about the first time you felt the power and presence of God's love touch your life.

Dynamic: The Mighty Power in Jesus Christ

Aside from personal subjective ways, there are objective historical and biblical facts that establish the uniqueness of the Lord Jesus Christ. He was and is unlike any other religious or spiritual leader.

His *Life* Was Unprecedented

Match the following verses with the correct descriptions by drawing lines to the correct statements:

1. Matthew 1:23	He was born of a virgin.
2. Matthew 20:28	He lived a sinless life.
3. Matthew 25:31-34	He willingly died a sacrificial death for human sin.
4. Matthew 28:5-7	He arose again from the dead.
5. Matthew 28:18-20	He promised to return again as King.
6. John 14:6	He declared Himself to be the way, the truth and the life.
7. 2 Corinthians 5:21	The focus of His life's mission was all people on earth.

His *Teaching* Was Unparalleled

Match the following verses with the correct descriptions:

8. Matthew 10:29-31	His Source of revelation was God, His Father in heaven.
9. Matthew 11:29,30	He came to fulfill the Old Testament prophecies.
10. Luke 19:10	He expressed the love of God, denouncing all fear.
11. Luke 24:25-27	He revealed a holy Creator God in all His attributes.
12. John 5:24; 6:44; 14:2	He claimed to be the Son of God and God.
13. John 8:9-11	He came to seek and save a lost humanity.
14. John 8:28,29	He acknowledged, confronted and overcame the sin problem.
15. John 10:4,27	He provides hope and healing for life's suffering and challenges.
16. John 14:8,9	He offers salvation by grace, not by human effort or goodness.
17. Acts 26:18	He provides guidance and direction for daily living.
18. Ephesians 2:8	He promised a future life in heaven and escape from hell.
19. Hebrews 1:1-3	He clearly differentiated between light and darkness, between God and Satan.

His Long-Term *Influence* Is Unmatched

- Witness to His gospel *commenced* with disciples such as Thomas who was known as the doubter (see John 20:24-29).

- Witness to the gospel *continues* with missionaries such as William Carey (1761-1834) who is known as the father of modern missions.

- Witness to the world will be *completed* before the end of time as we know it. Jesus confirmed that fact when He declared that the gospel will be preached to all nations and then shall the end come.

Personal Testimony

In your personal experience, which Christian examples have made a great impact on you as effective communicators of the gospel (i.e, Billy Graham, personal friends, etc.)? Explain your choices.

Which facet of the uniqueness of Jesus Christ is personally meaningful to you and can be incorporated into your personal testimony when you witness?

Illustration: The Testimony of Ishwar Dayal

Driven by an unsatisfied spiritual hunger, my grandfather, Ishwar Dayal, left his family to spend six years as a yogi in the Himalayan mountains. His quest to find inner peace led him to explore all of the spiritual experiences India's religions could offer him. Totally disillusioned with what he discovered, he eventually gave up. Yogi Ishwar Dayal returned home to his wife and his son, who by then was seven years old. He shaved his long hair and beard and took up employment as a treasurer in the palace of the Maharajah of Dharbanga in Bihar, North India.

Soon after his return to the real world, while about his daily work he was attracted to a public meeting in an open-air marketplace. For the first time in his life, he was given the Gospel of John in the Hindi language by a German Lutheran missionary. He devoured its contents with a voracious spiritual appetite. Then followed more reading material provided by the missionary, triggering ongoing lively discussions. After a series of question-and-answer sessions, he came to the conclusion that the salvation he yearned for was to be found in Jesus Christ.

His conversion to Christianity resulted in a very fruitful evangelism ministry to thousands. Far more than that, he passed on a legacy of faith to his own family that eventually birthed new Christians, fifteen of whom committed themselves to a life of involvement in ministry to others.

The major factor in the conversion of Ishwar Dayal was his realization of the uniqueness of who Jesus is placed alongside what is offered by other religions.

Outline your own personal testimony, highlighting the unique work Christ has done in your life. Include the following in your testimony:

- Your religious upbringing;
- Particular aspects of your pre-Christian life that might be of human interest;
- How you saw God working in your life before you became a Christian;
- Factors that led up to your acceptance of Jesus Christ as Savior and Lord;
- How you actually accepted Jesus Christ.

Session 2

The Messengers

The Christian Witness

Introduction

The omnipotent, awesome God of the universe has an urgent message of hope for humanity—salvation through the Lord Jesus Christ. Yet the task of spreading this message with eternal implications has been turned over to ordinary believers.

In the Old Testament, there were radical prophets who were proclaiming the message of Jehovah God and were driven by a passion that considered even sacrifice of their lives a worthy demonstration of their commitment. Israel was called not just to be faithful to God, but also to be a light to the Gentiles (see Genesis 12:1-3; Isaiah 49:6).

In the New Testament, a motley crew of 12 disciples—fishermen, a tax collector, businessmen and an anti-government extremist—equipped with the message of God's love in Christ and empowered by the Holy Spirit launched the Church throughout the whole world.

Today, despite living in a highly politicized society in which pluralism, multiculturalism and relativism are of supreme importance, the Christian is called to surrender—to die to one's self spiritually. Unless this happens, Christ cannot live through us in the power of the Holy Spirit and we cannot be effective witnesses.

Objective

Last session we considered the message of Christ. In this session we will explore the role of His messengers. Consider afresh His calling to us, His gifts for us, His personal preparation of us, His challenges to us and His power provided in us. Examine the eternal significance of the Church's eleventh-hour mission to invade the lives of hell-bound people with the love and the light of the Lord Jesus Christ.

Key Verses

"And Jesus came and spoke to them, saying, 'All authority has been given to Me in heaven and on earth. Go therefore and make disciples of all the nations, baptizing them in the name of the Father and of the Son and of the Holy Spirit, teaching them to observe all things that I have commanded you; and lo, I am with you always, even to the end of the age.' " Matthew 28:18-20

Preparation

Pray

- ✞ Ask the Lord to renew your call to Him and to help you reflect on how you are fulfilling it. Allow a time for confession, cleansing and praise.
- ✞ Ask God to help class members understand and accept how every Christian is called by God to evangelize by word and deed.
- ✞ Ask God for fruitfulness in fulfilling His call to us to communicate the gospel to others.

Prepare

- ❑ Read through the material thoroughly.
- ❑ Based on your personal reflection and the knowledge of who will attend the class, anticipate questions that they might ask and how you might answer them scripturally.
- ❑ Think through all items in this session—questions for consideration or discussion to help you guide the class in the right direction and avoid sidetracks and fruitless discussion.
- ❑ For Session 2A: Photocopy student handout "Eternal Significance" (pp. 39-40).
- ❑ Provide one index card for each group member for "Solutions for Improving Personal Evangelism."
- ❑ For Session 2B: Photocopy student handouts "Servants or Superstars?" (pp. 41-42); "Strategy—Charting a Course" (p. 43) and **Option:** "Illustration: A Witness to the End" (p. 44).
- ❑ Provide Bibles, paper, pens or pencils for those who might need them.
- ❑ Make a copy of "The Messengers: The Christian Witness: Take Action" sheet (pp. 37-38) for each group member.

Practice

At the end of each session is a Take Action plan. Use it to summarize the session, go over the action plan with students and encourage them to follow through on the action plan. As the leader of the study, you are strongly encouraged to practice what is learned so that you can share from your experiences—both the successes and failures—to help stimulate discussion and edify the class, as well as set an example for them to follow.

Session 2A

Introduce the Session (10 Minutes)

- Pray that God will develop in each member an understanding of the call to be a personal witness and to have a love and a passion for reaching the lost.
- Welcome the class members. Ask members if they had an opportunity to share their testimony with anyone during the past week. Ask at least one volunteer who responds affirmatively to *briefly* share about their experiences.
- **Or:** Ask one or two volunteers to share their written personal testimonies.

Step 1: Eternal Significance (20 Minutes)

- Divide class into small groups of four to six.
- Give each student a copy of "Eternal Significance" and a pen or pencil.

Explain: **The gospel has eternal significance to the lives of believers and to those who receive the message of the gospel through us. The significance for us as believers is stated in 1 Peter 1:3-5 and for the unbelievers in 1 Peter 2:7-12. Let's read these verses.**

- Instruct students to take 10 minutes to individually complete their handouts and then discuss their responses in their small groups for the remaining 10 minutes.

  Correct answers for #4 are underlined below:

  a. He was born of the Holy Spirit (see Matthew 1:18,20,21; Luke 1:30-35), just as <u>we are born of the Spirit</u> (see John 3:5).
  b. He was baptized by John (see Matthew 3:13-17; Mark 1:9-11; Luke 3:21,22), just as <u>we need to be baptized</u> (see Matthew 28:19; Acts 2:38).
  c. He was the light (see John 8:12), just as <u>we are light</u> (see Matthew 5:14-16).
  d. He was called "the Apostle," or the sent one from God (see Hebrews 3:1), just as <u>He has sent us into the world</u> (see Matthew 28:18-20; Acts 1:8).

Option: Symbolism of the Messenger (10 Minutes)

- With the whole group give the following information, reading the scripture, and discussing as you go through the information.
- Begin by explaining:

  Throughout Scripture we find word pictures of our eternal significance as disciples of the Lord Jesus Christ.

➻ Discuss:
How do the following word pictures relate to being personal Christian witnesses?

Servant messenger—The servant messenger is described in **Isaiah 49:1-6**. In Bible days, the servant—often confused with the position of slave—was respected, remunerated for his or her services and responsive to the master. Scripture has several examples of those who were called from birth to fulfill God's mission, i.e., Moses, John the Baptist, etc.

Light—In the Sermon on the Mount (see **Matthew 5:14-16**) we see the path of spiritual light moving in the following manner:

- Having inner light in your own life;
- Bringing light to your own household;
- Bringing light to the rest of the city.

Salt—**Matthew 5:13** warns that if salt loses its savor, it is only worthy, or fit, to be trodden under the feet of men.

Ambassadors—An ambassador is a representative of the authority of a king, prime minister or the government of a nation (see **2 Corinthians 5:20**).

➻ Discuss (suggested answer in parentheses):
Paul states that he is "not ashamed of the gospel of Christ, for it is the power of God to salvation" (Romans 1:16). Why was Paul not ashamed of the gospel? (He was totally confident in the message of the gospel; he knew God provided the power to convert and bring full salvation to all who believe.)

Option: Substitutes for Personal Evangelism (15 Minutes)

➻ Explain: **Sometimes we as Christians will do anything to avoid personally witnessing to others. It is not uncommon for Christians to get sidetracked from the eternal significance of personal evangelism.** Ask students to think about what they do instead of personally witnessing. As they share, write their responses on the board, overhead or newsprint.

➻ **Some common substitutes for our personal involvement and fulfillment as witnesses include** (write the following list on the board, overhead or newsprint as you explain):

- **Giving financially to missions;**
- **Giving to build church buildings and programs;**
- **Giving money to charity to feed the hungry and poor;**
- **Supporting mass evangelism ventures;**
- **Witnessing together in groups as Christians.**

➻ Explain: **Although each of these actions is good and has a place in serving others, it does not absolve us from our personal responsibility to witness to others.** Discuss the following:

1. **What are some other substitutes Christians may use in place of personal witnessing?** Add their responses to the previous list.
2. **What substitutes have you used, or are currently using, to avoid witnessing personally to non-Christians?**

Step 2: Stumbling Blocks to Personal Evangelism (10 Minutes)

➻ Explain: **In surveying Christians over the years, several stumbling blocks continue to surface as reasons for our negligence in sharing Christ personally with others. What are some stumbling blocks that keep us from sharing Christ with the lost?**

➻ As group members share, write their responses on a white board, overhead transparency or newsprint, filling in any of the following that are not mentioned.

- Fear of personal rejection
- Feelings of inadequacy
- Spiritual lukewarmness from living in the comfort zone
- Busyness
- Lack of biblical knowledge
- Believing that nobody is interested in the gospel message
- Bad experiences in the past
- Fear of getting involved in spiritual warfare
- Few role models

Step 3: Solutions for Improving Personal Evangelism (5-10 Minutes)

- Explain: **Personal spiritual disciplines are necessary to developing the lifestyle of a Christan witness.**
- Ask the whole group: **What disciplines are needed in order to be a dynamic personal witness?**
- As group members respond to the question, list their responses on the board, overhead or newsprint. Be sure the following disciplines are mentioned:

  - Regular personal Bible study and prayer;
  - Exercising faith and seeing the rewards of that faith for daily challenges;
  - Action, translating your good intentions into actively reaching out to the lost and sharing with them the message of the gospel of Jesus Christ.

- Challenge group members to examine their lives for the ways that they avoid being personal witnesses, and for which spiritual disciplines they need to apply to their lives.
- Give each group member an index card. Ask each one to commit to *one* step he or she will take this week to improve his or her personal witnessing. Instruct them to write their names at the top of their cards and write their commitments. Then instruct them to trade cards with another group member and commit to pray for one another during the week.

Two-Meeting Track: If you want to spread the session over two meetings, stop here and close in prayer. Inform students of the content to be covered in your next meeting.

Session 2B

PREPARATION

Pray

- ✞ Ask God to show you what He wants you to learn about being one of His messengers.
- ✞ Ask God to prepare the hearts of the class members to clearly understand and fulfill their roles as servant-witnesses.
- ✞ Ask God to pour His spirit of servanthood through each one who shares a personal witness this week so that unbelievers sense and respond to the humility of Jesus Christ.

Prepare

- ❑ Photocopy student handouts "Servants or Superstars?" (pp. 41-42), "Strategy—Charting a Course" (p. 43) and **Option:** "Illustration: A Witness to the End" (p. 44).
- ❑ Carefully read through the lesson on "Servants or Superstars?" If your time is limited, you may have to condense or skip some of the information.
- ❑ Provide Bibles, paper, pens or pencils for those who might need them.

INTRODUCE THE SESSION (10 MINUTES)

- ✞ Begin the session by praying that this lesson will give group members the desire to develop servants' hearts for the lost.
- ➼ Give members two minutes to share with their prayer partners the results of their commitment made at the end of the last session.
- ➼ Ask volunteers to share some of the stumbling blocks/solutions for personal evangelism from the last session. Ask if anyone used the information or changed an attitude or action as a result of the last session.
- 💡 Ask at least one volunteer to share his or her written personal testimony.

STEP 4: SERVANTS OR SUPERSTARS? (30-45 MINUTES)

- ➼ Give each group member the notetaking page for "Servants or Superstars?"
- ➼ Present the following information to the whole group.

Explain: **People who overcome impossible odds and accomplish a great mission are often hailed as superstars. In the Bible we see how God prepared "messenger models" who displayed a spirit of servanthood, even as they accomplished their divinely ordained mission. Keep this in mind as we study the following messengers of God:**

1. **Abraham** strove to save his immediate family out of Sodom and Gomorrah (from **Genesis 18—19**). The following should be noted:

    - The spiritual bankruptcy of Sodom and Gomorrah (see 18:20,21; 19:4-9);
    - The prayer of Abraham to God to spare Sodom and Gomorrah if there were enough righteous people (see 18:23-33);
    - Divine intervention was necessary to deliver his nephew Lot and Lot's family (see 19:1,2,10,11,15-29).

2. About **Noah** (from **Genesis 6—8**), the following should be noted:

    - He lived in a callous generation (see 6:5,12);
    - The certainty of judgment (see 6:7,13);
    - Noah's commitment, faith, perseverance and hope to share the message before it was too late (see 6:8,22; 7:1,5; 8:1,6-22);
    - Jesus also commented that prior to His return the days would be similar to the days of Noah (see Matthew 24:36-39).

3. Summarizing **Joseph**'s life (from **Genesis 37—50**), he was:

    - A victim persecuted by his own family (see 37:3,4,12-36);
    - A vessel who was seduced by Potiphar's wife but chose to serve God faithfully (see 39:1-23);
    - A victor who ultimately triumphed because of his faith in God and as a strong witness of God's power in his life (see 39:1-6,20-23; 40:1-22; 41:1-57; 45:3-25).

4. **Moses**' life (from Exodus 2—19) can be summarized in the following manner:

    - He refused to identify with Egypt despite the royal status given to him (see Exodus 2:11);
    - He had a burning bush experience in which he encountered the great "I AM"—the God of Abraham, Isaac and Jacob (see Exodus 3:1-22);
    - He used supernatural demonstrations to bring redemption to God's people (see Exodus 4:27-31; 7:1-20; 14:13-31).

5. Summarizing **Daniel**'s personal witness (from the book of **Daniel**), please note the following:

    - Babylon was filled with witchcraft and all kinds of occult practices (see Daniel 2:2).
    - Daniel had an excellent spirit in the middle of his circumstances (see Daniel 1:8-13; 6:3-5,10-12).
    - Despite the privileges given to him and under penalty of death, he refused to worship an image of the king, but rather chose to continue to honor the one true God (see Daniel 6:10-13).

6. Note **Shadrach, Meshach** and **Abednego** (from **Daniel 1 and 3**):

    - They had the choice to bow or to burn (see 3:1-18);
    - Note that Jesus was with them in the fiery furnace (see 3:24,25);
    - Their faithfulness ultimately resulted in a strong witness on behalf of Jehovah God (see 3:26-30).

7. Reviewing **John the Baptist**'s life (from the **New Testament Gospels**), note the following:

    - He was a mouthpiece to announce the coming of the Lord Jesus Christ (see Matthew 3:1-3,11,12).
    - He openly condemned sin to the point of being beheaded for his bold declaration of truth (see Mark 6:17-29).
    - He acknowledged, despite his strong ministry, that Jesus Christ was in fact the Lamb of God who would take away the sins of the world (see John 1:24-34).

In the preceding examples of personal witness, the servant's heart comes through loud and clear. Think of someone you know who needs you to be salt and light to him or her. Now consider practical ways in which you can be a servant to that person, thereby creating a platform for you to share the "truth in love."

➻ Give group members a minute or two to write down practical ways to serve another person.

Step 5: Strategy—Charting a Course (15 Minutes)

- Divide students into groups of four or five. Appoint a leader for each group.
- Instruct small group leaders to assign the listed passages to group members to be read aloud.
- Have the small groups discuss their answers to the question on the handout.

The following are the main points of each passage.

1. **Search your heart—Luke 14:1-14:** Examine your attitudes toward others; avoid legalism and self-importance. Love and serve others in humility.
2. **Seek the lost—Luke 19:10:** Jesus Christ came to seek and to save the lost. A Christian witness must begin by looking for lost people.
3. **Sensitivity for the lost—Luke 15:1-10:** A Christian witness must be compassionate toward the lost.
4. **Surrender to Christ—Luke 9:23-26; 14:25-33:** As the Lord provides, a Christian witness must be willing to invest the time, the money and the expression of his/her talent needed to bring light to the lost.

- After about 12 minutes, bring the whole group back together and share the following information, asking them to write the points on their handouts:

  Now is an opportune time to witness because:

  - **People are ignorant of what the Bible really says, about who God is and what He can do in their lives; yet many want to know.**
  - **People have reaped the results of their own sin and many of them are ready to turn to God.**
  - **We live in the days of final opportunity for the Holy Spirit to convict the world of sin, righteousness and judgment (see John 16:9-11). Jesus stated that the harvest is plenteous and that the time for salvation is now (see Matthew 9:37).**

Option: Illustration: A Witness to the End (15 Minutes)

- Divide students into groups of four or five.
- Give each student a copy of "Illustration: A Witness to the End."
- Have the small groups read the illustration and discuss the questions.

Take Action

- Give each member a copy of the Take Action page. Discuss with the whole group. Encourage them to take the actions suggested.

The Christian Witness

Take Action

Session Summary

The Christian believer has been called to be a light in this dark world. God's gifts and calling are without a recall notice. Just as God the Father sent Jesus His Son, He in turn sends out His disciples to be His light in the sin-darkened world. The Christian can be pictured in various ways, such as light, salt and an ambassador to the world.

It is easy to withdraw into a comfortable level by developing substitutes for personally sharing our faith with others. We all face challenges to personal witnessing. The Bible is filled with examples that are both instructional and inspirational. To be successful witnesses, both an attitude of surrender and a workable strategy are essential. God knows those who are ready to respond and can lead us to them.

Action Plan for the Week

1. Memorize Matthew 28:18-20 by writing it on a 3x5-inch card and putting it in a prominent place where you will see it frequently.

2. Ask the Lord to point out the substitutes and/or excuses you use to avoid personally witnessing to those whom you encounter on a daily or weekly basis. What can you do to reach out to at least one person this week to let him or her know about God's loving plan?

3. Begin to compile a list of the unsaved with whom you come in contact and begin to pray for those on your list.

4. If you traded a commitment card to work on one step toward improving your personal witness, pray for the class member with whom you traded cards. Don't forget to follow through on your own commitment step.

Closing Prayer

Father,

Thank You for the gifts and calling You have placed in my life. Please forgive me for any substitutes to which I have resorted to avoid personal witnessing. I surrender to Your Holy Spirit and pray that You will lead me to those who are ready and waiting to respond to the message of Your salvation through the Lord Jesus Christ. In His name, I pray. Amen.

Eternal Significance

The Calling

1. Please read the following statements and write "agree" or "disagree" beside each one:

__________ The calling of God to be personal witnesses is only for the clergy.

__________ The source of the calling to be personal witnesses is the Church.

__________ The calling to be a personal witness is from God to every Christian as part of His master plan to redeem the people.

Discuss the following:

2. Scripture clearly confirms that He who has called us, referring to God, is faithful to accomplish the work to which He has called us (see 1 Thessalonians 5:24). Elaborate on your understanding of what it means when it is stated that God will help you fulfill your calling.

3. Scripture indicates that people cannot hear the gospel of Jesus Christ "without a preacher" (see Romans 10:14). Briefly explain what this verse means to you, and the role of the individual in personal witnessing.

4. Also note that before the final close of time, John pictures representatives from every tribe and nation of the earth en masse before God's throne (see Revelation 7:9,10). Utilizing this information, discuss the significance and scope of being a personal witness.

The supreme example before us as a personal witness is the Lord Jesus Christ Himself. Scripture states that Jesus, as part of His commission to His disciples, stated that even as the Father sent Him, so He has sent us (see John 20:21,22). Complete the following statements:

a. He was born of the Holy Spirit (see Matthew 1:18,20,21; Luke 1:30-35), just as

____

(see John 3:5).

b. He was baptized by John (see Matthew 3:13-17; Mark 1:9-11; Luke 3:21,22), just as _______________________________________ (see Matthew 28:19; Acts 2:38).

c. He was the light (see John 8:12), just as

____

(see Matthew 5:14-16).

d. He was called "the Apostle," or the sent one from God (see Hebrews 3:1), just as

____

(see Matthew 28:18-20; Acts 1:8).

5. If every Christian is to be sent in the same manner as the Lord Jesus Christ, how do the preceding scriptural facts relate to us being personal witnesses?

Servants or Superstars?

The Bible has many examples of messengers.

1. Abraham (Genesis 18—19)

2. Noah (Genesis 6—8)

3. Joseph (Genesis 37—50)

4. Moses (Exodus 2—19)

5. Daniel (the book of Daniel)

6. Shadrach, Meshach and Abednego (Daniel 1 and 3)

7. John the Baptist

   a. Matthew 3:1-3,11,12

   b. Mark 6:17-29

   c. John 1:24-34

In the preceding examples of personal witness, the servant's heart comes through loud and clear. Think of someone you know who needs you to be "salt and light" to him or her. Now consider practical ways in which you can be a servant to that person, thereby creating a platform for you to share the "truth in love."

Strategy—Charting a Course

Read the following Scripture references and discuss the questions.

1. **Search your heart**—Read Luke 14:1-14.
   What is Jesus teaching in this passage about our attitudes toward others?

2. **Seek the lost**—Luke 19:10
   Think about the people you interact with on a day-to-day basis. Who are the lost that Jesus came for in your neighborhood, at work, among your family and friends? Give specific names.

   As an ambassador of Christ, what is God calling you to do in your relationship with the people you have named?

3. **Sensitivity for the lost**—Luke 15:1-10
   What do these parables teach about the urgency of reaching the lost? What should we be doing to reach them?

4. **Surrender to Christ**—Luke 9:23-26; 14:25-33
   What has it cost you to be a committed Christian? What will it cost you to be a dynamic personal witness for Christ in terms of money, emotion, logistics, relationships, reputation, etc.? Be specific.

Now is an opportune time to witness because:

-
-
-

Illustration: A Witness to the End

For several years now, a true story has been circulating in some Christian publications, concerning the conversion of a lost soul in a Russian prison. For many decades, prior to the fall of the communist regime in the former Soviet Union, many were imprisoned for speaking out boldly against communism, as well as for the Lord Jesus Christ. We are told that a prisoner, in the final moments of his life, despite his persecution and his ill health, was able to witness to a fellow prisoner in the cell adjacent to his. Shortly after sharing that witness and leading his fellow prisoner to Christ, he died.

The new convert was Aleksandr Solzhenitsyn, who was not only an advocate for freedom and hope in the Soviet Union, but also a strong Christian witness who shares the light of political freedom *and* spiritual freedom through the gospel in his own nation and around the world.

Not every convert we lead to the Lord Jesus Christ will become that famous or of such high profile. However, we also never know on this side of heaven how impactful our witness will be.

1. Who first told you the gospel message? How did you respond at first?

2. With whom have you recently shared Christ? What was the response?

   If you have not shared Christ with someone recently, in retrospect when did the opportunity arise? Why did you not make the most of it?

   How can you make opportunities to witness?

3. Who in your life needs the love of God in Christ Jesus? What will you do to give them the opportunity to choose?

Session 3

The Masses

Who Is the Spiritual Harvest?

Introduction

Who is the harvest? It is a question few Christians ask. Even fewer seek to answer the question. In a customer sensitive economy, billions are spent annually to pinpoint and provide for the felt needs of product buyers, but precious little is spent on identifying and reaching people who are lost without Christ.

Estimates are that only 10 percent of Christians witness regularly and almost 50 percent of Christians have never introduced a soul to Jesus Christ. Most Christians, after three years in the Church, have in fact insulated themselves from socializing with any non-Christians, thereby making them ineffective witnesses. We have, in fact, isolated ourselves from our "customers" with the result that what the masses think and believe is even further removed from us and our beliefs.

Unfortunately, evangelism to many Christians has primarily come to mean inviting non-Christians to large-scale evangelistic events such as concerts and crusades. When blessed by the Holy Spirit, these evangelistic events are effective, but by becoming overly dependent upon this format for witnessing, we have missed something very precious and valuable—that is, being personally involved in the lives of non-Christians and in the process of leading them to salvation. Granted, Jesus did address the multitudes on various occasions, but His primary and most effective method of communicating the Good News was in small groups and in one-on-one conversations, customizing His message to each individual.

Objective

Who really is our target audience? This session profiles the masses, then it shows how Jesus approached various types of people in a variety of ways and how to use His approach for reaching the spiritually hungry.

Key Verse

"Lift up your eyes and look at the fields, for they are already white for harvest!"
John 4:35

Preparation

Pray

- ✝ Ask God to show you what bridges you need to build to the unbelievers in your sphere of influence.
- ✝ Ask God to make each one in your group pliable and open to building bridges to their lost neighbors.
- ✝ Ask God to bless with fruit the efforts of you and your students as you build bridges to the lost.

Prepare

- ❑ Read through the material thoroughly. Practice presenting "Statistics and Trends" (pp. 47-49) until you are comfortable with the material.
- ❑ Based on your personal reflection and the knowledge of who will attend the class, anticipate questions that they might ask and how you might answer them scripturally.
- ❑ Think through all items in this session—questions for consideration or discussion to help you guide the class in the right direction and avoid sidetracks and fruitless discussion.
- ❑ For Session 3A: Photocopy student handouts "Statistics and Trends" (pp. 55-56); "Hindrances to Evangelism" (pp. 57-58); **Option:** "Types of Non-Christians" (p. 61) and **Option:** "Bridging the Gulf" (pp. 59-60).
- ❑ For Session 3B: Photocopy student handouts "The Jesus Model" (pp. 62-63); **Option:** "Response to the Gospel" (pp. 64-65) and **Option:** "Illustration: Whose Agenda—Yours or God's?" (p. 66).
- ❑ Provide Bibles, paper, pens or pencils for those who might need them.
- ❑ Make a copy of "The Masses: Who Is the Spiritual Harvest: Take Action" (pp. 53-54) for each group member.

Practice

At the end of each session is a Take Action plan. Use it to summarize the session, go over the action plan with students and encourage them to follow through on the action plan. As the leader of the study, you are strongly encouraged to practice what is learned so that you can share from your experiences—both the successes and failures—to help stimulate discussion and edify the class, as well as set an example for them to follow.

Session 3A

Introduce the Session (10 Minutes)

- ✞ Pray that group members will be empowered by the Holy Spirit to be effective sowers, waterers and reapers of the lost as a result of this session.
- ➻ Welcome the members. Ask them to share things they have heard in the news that reflect the spiritual climate in the United States.
- ➻ Ask one or two volunteers to share their personal testimonies.

Step 1: Statistics and Trends (30 Minutes)

- ➻ Give each group member a copy of the note-taking pages "Statistics and Trends."
- ➻ Present the following information and discuss any questions that arise.

Worldwide Statistics

Statistics are not gospel truth. They are mere numbers that are subject to different interpretations; they can be manipulated to suit different purposes and they change over time. They may, however, offer the opportunity to discern some realistic facts and offer some direction.

David B. Barrett, currently Honorable Research Advisor for the United Bible Societies and Research Professor of Missiometrics at Regent University, is a world-respected Christian statistician. He figures that as of mid-1998:

- 33.2 percent of the world's population of 5.9 billion people identify themselves as Christians (1.966 billion);
- 19.9 percent as Muslims (1.179 billion);
- 12.9 percent as Hindus (767.4 million);
- 12.9 percent as nonreligious (766.7 million);
- 6.0 percent as Buddhists (356.9 million);
- 4.1 percent as tribal religionists (244.1 million);
- 2.5 percent as atheists (146.4 million);
- 1.7 percent as new-age religionists (99.1 million);
- less than 1 percent Sikhs (22.8 million); and
- less than 1 percent Jews (15.1 million).[1]

Explain: **Keep in mind that for the purpose of Barrett's studies he defines "Christians" not as "authentic born-again believers" (who are known with certainty only to God). Rather, Barrett's category of "Christians" includes all *professing* Christians and their children, *secret believers* as well as those who**

for various reasons are *unaffiliated* with recognized Christian churches. Clearly even among those who think of themselves as "Christian" in some sense, there is much evangelistic work to be done.

But what about those people who live in cultural/language groups where there is little or no Christian presense of any sort—"unreached people groups"? The U.S. Center for World Mission in Pasadena, California, estimates that there are still 8000 people *groups* in the world that have *no access to a viable church,* and therefore very little opportunity to even *hear* the gospel.

"God shows no partiality" (Acts 10:34). The Bible clearly teaches that God loves everyone whom He has created (see John 3:16). So whether people come from Christian, post-Christian, or non-Christian people groups or lands, one thing is certain: God is "not willing that any should perish but that all should come to repentance" (2 Peter 3:9).

Trends in the United States

Statistics on the Church in the United States during the 80s and 90s have not been particularly encouraging. **On the one hand surveys consistently show that about 28 percent (75 million out of a population of 265 million) claim to be born again. Yet statistics also show that...**

- Church attendance is declining.[2]
- Those who do attend church are accepting other non-Christian religious ideologies and values.[3]
- The behavior of church attenders on a wide range of issues, from cheating to divorce, is becoming indistinguishable from that of non-believers.[4]
- Where churches *are* growing it is usually as a result of people leaving smaller churches and switching to larger ones, rather than churches growing as a result of evangelizing the unchurched.[5]

Who Is the Harvest?

Obviously, the Church has its work cut out for it to *disciple* those who claim to be born again. But what about the other 190 million Americans who are not born from above as Jesus taught Nicodemus in John 3? Who are included in this vast potential harvest? Those who...

- **Believe in other world religions;**
- **Are involved in the cults;**
- **Do not hold any specific religious beliefs.**

Explain: The first two of these three groups are relatively small, even though most of the efforts of Christian apologists (those who make an intellectual defense of Christian faith) over the past thirty years have concentrated on them. But for the vast majority, those who have no specific religious commitments, relatively little effort has been exerted.

The astonishing truth is that these 120-150 million Americans represent a huge block of people, a block of people nearly as unevangelized, and in every bit as much spiritual peril, as Muslims, Hindus, Buddhists and those who practice tribal religions! These are our neighbors, coworkers, and sometimes people we share a pew with every Sunday morning. These are the harvest that we are called to share Christ with.

Step 2: Hindrances to Evangelism (10-15 Minutes)

- Give each member a copy of the note-taking page "Hindrances to Evangelism."
- Discuss each of the following items so that there is a clear understanding of the issues and encourage students to fill in the blanks or take notes. Use the questions at the end for discussion.

There are many problems that bog us down as Christian witnesses.

- Our priorities have been reshuffled. The mechanics of the program or the method have become more important than our mission to seek and save the lost.
- We preach divine principles with little emphasis on divine presence and thereby become legalistic and judgmental based upon appearance or behavior, rather than open to all kinds of people wherever they are in life.
- We think we have it right when we say the "right" words or use the right method, rather than seeking to become the message with our whole lives.
- Personal witnessing has not been modeled by pastors and ministers. Often relegated to the minister of evangelism, evangelism becomes a process of calling on newcomers and visitors to the church.
- Discipleship and personal witnessing have been presented as an option rather than a divine mandate.
- Christians are often intimidated and fearful of the world.
- Personal witnessing in many churches is looked upon as a program, not a lifestyle.
- As a whole, many churches have forgotten the source of power for personal witnessing—the Holy Spirit.

- We have become defenders of the faith, rather than sharers of the faith.
- We have allowed our church's agenda to be human driven, rather than Spirit empowered and directed.
- There is very little "show and tell" evangelism. In fact many seminaries and Bible colleges do not even require a course on personal witnessing for ministers in training.
- We often buy into the trap of "respecting others' rights" and decide not to witness to others, rather than take the chance of offending someone.

1. There may be other stumbling blocks and traps as well. List others that have not been included in the above list.
2. What traps have ensnared you? Your church?

Option: Bridging the Gulf (10 Minutes)

- ➻ Give each student a copy of "Bridging the Gulf."
- ➻ Instruct them to take the handout home, read it and answer the questions. **Or:** Give the students a few minutes of class time to complete the handout.

Option: Types of Non-Christians (10-20 Minutes)

- ➻ Divide the class into three fairly equal-sized groups.
- ➻ Give each group a copy of "Types of Non-Christians." Assign one of the situations to each group to brainstorm ideas for witnessing to the person described.
- ➻ Have each group choose two members to role-play their suggestions for the whole class.
- **Option:** If you choose not to do the role play, bring the groups back together to share their ideas with the other small groups, telling them: **Brainstorm ideas and be prepared to share your best ideas with the whole group.**

Two-Meeting Track: If you want to spread this session over two meetings, stop here and close in prayer. Inform students of the content to be covered in your next meeting.

Session 3B

Preparation

Pray

- Ask God to teach you from Jesus' model of witnessing.
- Ask God to make the class members excited and willing to practice the Jesus model of witnessing.
- Ask God to bless the group efforts with fruitfulness as each member attempts to follow the example of Jesus.

Prepare

- ❑ Photocopy student handouts "The Jesus Model," (pp. 62-63); **Option:** "Response to the Gospel" (pp. 64-65) and **Option:** "Illustration: Whose Agenda—Yours or God's?" (p. 66).

Introduce the Session (10 Minutes)

- Welcome students.
- Ask one or two volunteers to share their personal testimonies.
- Discuss: **What statistic or fact that we discussed during the last session was most surprising to you?**
- Or discuss: **What is the greatest hindrance to personal evangelism in our own church?**

Step 3: The Jesus Model (20-30 Minutes)

- Divide class members into small groups of four to six members.
- Give each member a copy of "The Jesus Model" and a pen or pencil.
- Have the groups discuss the questions on the handout.

Option: Response to the Gospel (15 Minutes)

- Give each group member a copy of "Response to the Gospel."
- Discuss the questions with the whole group. **Or:** Have class members remain in their small groups to discuss the questions. For question 2 assign each Scripture passage to a different group member to read aloud, then ask group members to share their responses.

Option: Illustration: Whose Agenda—Yours or God's? (15 Minutes)

- Give each member a copy of "Illustration: Whose Agenda—Yours or God's?"
- Read the story aloud and discuss the questions as a group.

Take Action

- Give each member a copy of the Take Action page. Discuss with the whole group. Encourage them to take the actions suggested.

Notes:

1. Derived from statistics in an article by David B. Barrett and Todd M. Johnson, "Annual Statistical Table on Global Mission: 1998," *International Bulletin of Missionary Research* 22, No. 1 (1998): 26,27.
2. George Barna, *Virtual America: The Barna Report 1994-95* (Ventura, CA: Regal Books, 1994), p. 47.
3. Ibid., pp. 114-117.
4. Ibid., p. 146.
5. George Barna, *User Friendly Churches* (Ventura, CA: Regal Books, 1991), pp. 19-20.

Who Is the Spiritual Harvest?

Take Action

Session Summary

In this session we have identified our target audience within the masses. We have shared both worldwide and U.S. statistics and trends concerning unbelievers. We have defined who the harvest really is in the U.S. We have pinpointed hindrances and problems that deter us from the course of witnessing effectively. We have cited the importance of building bridges between Christian witnesses and unbelievers. Biblical models definitively highlighting the Jesus model have been shared with the hope that the insights we gain will provide instruction and inspiration to be effective witnesses. We have been reminded about the fact that some sow, others water and others reap. The results and fruitfulness come from God Himself.

Action Plan for the Week

1. Memorize John 4:35 by writing it on a 3x5-inch index card and post it in a prominent place where you can read it often.

2. Continue to add to your prayer list of unsaved relatives, friends and acquaintances and remember to pray for them.

3. Specifically ask God to bring an opportunity this week for you to begin to share your life and witness with one of the people on your prayer list.

Closing Prayer

Father in heaven,

I acknowledge that I live in a world with many lost people. Not just lost people overseas, but lost people right in my own neighborhood. Help me as a member of Your Church to both discern and deal with the stumbling blocks and problems that bog me down as an effective witness. Help me to take initiative to bridge the gulf between non-Christians and myself. Give me an open heart to learn from the biblical approaches and the Jesus model of personal witnessing. Give me creativity by the power of the Holy Spirit to consider each non-Christian I know and prayerfully decide the best approach to reach each one with Your message. I fully recognize that nothing or anything I can do is effective without the power of the Holy Spirit. Allow me the privilege of sowing, watering and/or reaping as part of Your master plan. Help me to be an effective Christian witness. In Jesus' name, I pray. Amen.

Statistics and Trends

Worldwide Statistics

Statistics are not gospel truth. They are mere numbers that are subject to different interpretations; they can be manipulated to suit different purposes; and they change over time. They may, however, offer the opportunity to discern some realistic facts and offer some direction.

David B. Barrett, currently Honorable Research Advisor for the United Bible Societies and Research Professor of Missiometrics at Regent University, is a world-respected Christian statistician. He figures that as of mid-1998...

- ________________ of the world's population of 5.9 billion people identify themselves as Christians (1.966 billion)
- ________________ as Muslims (1.179 billion)
- ________________ as Hindus (767.4 million)
- ________________ as nonreligious (766.7 million)
- ________________ as Buddhists (356.9 million)
- ________________ as tribal religionists (244.1 million)
- ________________ as atheists (146.4 million)
- ________________ as New Age religionists (99.1 million)
- less than ________________ Sikhs (22.8 million)
- less than ________________ Jews (15.1 million)

Notes

Trends in the United States

Statistics on the Church in the United States during the 80s and 90s have not been particularly encouraging.

- Church attendence is ____.
- Those who do attend church are ____
____.
- The behavior of church attenders on a wide range of issues, from cheating to divorce, is ____.
- Where churches *are* growing it is usually as a result of people ____ and ____, rather than churches growing as a result ____.

Who Is the Harvest?

Obviously, the church has its work cut out for it to *disciple* those who claim to be born again. But what about the other 190 million Americans who are not born from above as Jesus taught Nicodemus in John 3? Who are included in this vast potential harvest? Those who...

-
-
-

Notes

Hindrances to Evangelism

There are many problems that bog us down as Christian witnesses:

- Our priorities have been ______________. The mechanics of the program or the method have become more important than our mission to seek and save the lost.
- We preach divine ______________ with little emphasis on divine ______________ and thereby become legalistic and judgmental based upon appearance or behavior, rather than open to all kinds of people wherever they are in life.
- We think we have it right when we say the ______________ ______________ or use the ______________ ______________, rather than seeking to ______________ the message with our whole lives.
- Personal witnessing has not been ______________ by pastors and ministers. Often relegated to the minister of evangelism, evangelism becomes a process of ______________ ______________ newcomers and visitors to the church.
- Discipleship and personal witnessing have been presented as an ______________ rather than a divine ______________.
- Christians are often ______________ and ______________ of the world.
- Personal witnessing in many churches is looked upon as a ______________, not a ______________.
- As a whole, many churches have forgotten the______________ of ______________ for personal witnessing—the Holy Spirit.
- We have become ______________ of the faith, rather than of the faith.
- We have allowed our church's agenda to be ______________ ______________, rather than Spirit ______________ and ______________.
- There is very little "______________ and ______________" evangelism. In fact many seminaries and Bible colleges do not even require a course on personal witnessing for ministers in training.
- We often buy into the trap of "______________ others' ______________" and decide not to witness to others, rather than take the chance of ______________ someone.

1. There may be other stumbling blocks and traps as well. List others that have not been included in the above list.

2. What traps have ensnared you?

   Your church?

Bridging the Gulf

To reach our non-Christian friends, relatives, coworkers and neighbors with the gospel, we need to take the initiative to bridge the gulf between our church culture and their unchurched culture.

Communication

Listening is as important as talking. We love to fellowship with other Christians, but it takes effort, commitment and a love for the lost to talk with people who are different from us. They have different goals and desires, different family backgrounds and different interests. Yet they still need a witness of the Lord Jesus Christ.

Storytelling

Proclaiming the gospel is not just enumerating abstract truths; it is telling stories about how God has come through for us. We need to use stories that serve as windows into the kingdom of God. Illustrations help clarify what we are talking about. Many Christians have forgotten that Jesus was a master storyteller. His parables illustrated spiritual truths with simple everyday examples.

Closeness to God

The power of Christian witness is energized by a person who witnesses dynamically by the Holy Spirit and is able to share vibrant personal testimony of his or her current involvement with God Himself. It is this that excites others, specifically non-Christians who will be challenged as well to trust God to meet their daily needs and to answer their prayers.

Many times we as Christians have lost our "connection" with God and need to reestablish that before we can be effective witnesses to the lost.

1. Evaluate: What is your personal witnessing style?

_______________ a. Are you a natural storyteller like Jesus (see Matthew 13:1-23)?
_______________ b. Are you a bold proclaimer of the gospel like Paul (see Acts 17:22-34)?
_______________ c. Are you a powerful role model through faithful action like Stephen (see Acts 7:54-60).
_______________ d. Are you a ready ambassador like Philip (see Acts 8:26-39)?
_______________ e. Are you good at giving a personal testimony like Mary Magdalene and the other Mary (see Matthew 28:1-10)?
_______________ f. ______________________________
(Write in your own biblical example.)

2. In which of these areas of personal witnessing are you weak?

Pray:

Heavenly Father,

Thank You for all the gifts You have given me to be an ambassador of Jesus Christ. I give myself to You to use me as a witness to share the Good News with the lost. Please strengthen me in areas in which I need courage and practice, for You say in Your Word that in my weakness You are strong (see 2 Corinthians 12:9). In Jesus' name, amen.

Types of Non-Christians

Read the descriptions of the following situations. How would you approach each person in sharing Christ?

1. A motel owner who came to the United States with a few dollars in his pocket built a successful business. Coming from a Hindu background, he contributed to the building of two Hindu temples in northern California. He also got in touch with others from his native India and encouraged them to contribute. The motel owner, when presented the gospel message of Jesus Christ, said that he believed that all religions were the same, and he had respect for Christ and Christianity, as well as other religious leaders and religions. He did not want to make any commitment that would hurt his financial income and success.

2. A young lady whom I met at a convention works for a large company selling copiers. When I shared the gospel with her, she was moved to tears. Many Christians around her had insisted on immediate conversion, and she felt that her needs were really not being addressed. The lady, with tears in her eyes, said she was sincerely seeking and searching, but she did not fully understand what it meant to be a Christian. She was fearful of being rushed into a decision she would later regret.

3. On an airplane I met another gentleman who was quite restless and seemed upset about something. When I asked him how he was doing, he seemed reluctant to open up any part of his life.

The Jesus Model

Jesus witnessed to Nicodemus. Carefully read John 3:1-21 and answer the following questions:

1. Who was Nicodemus?

2. When did he come to see Jesus?

   What is significant about the time of day that he came to visit Jesus (see v. 2)?

3. What was the message Jesus shared with him?

4. Why did Jesus share the mysteries of the work of the Holy Spirit?

Read John 4:1-42 and answer the following questions:

5. What is unique about the timing of this conversation?

6. How did Jesus express acceptance to the Samaritan woman?

7. How did Jesus get in touch with her inner feelings?

8. What symbolism did He use?

9. Describe the prophetic insight Jesus shared to make her open to the gospel.

10. How did she try to sidetrack Jesus when He confronted her sin?

11. What statement indicates that she did recognize that Jesus was the answer?

12. What did Jesus say was His spiritual meat and nourishment?

13. What did Jesus specifically say about the harvest concerning the amount, the timing, the visibility, laborers and the importance of prayer?

14. The Jesus model was also followed by Paul. Read Acts 17:16-31 and discuss the following:

    a. What greatly distressed Paul?

    b. What verses indicated that Paul had a good feel for the search and the struggle of the Athenians?

    c. How did he show his understanding of the Athenian culture?

Response to the Gospel

1. What response should we expect from those to whom we witness? Read the parable of the soils in Matthew 13:1-23 and answer the following questions:

    a. Who is the sower?

    b. List the types of soil.

    c. What were some of the responses?

    d. What keeps people from receiving and accepting the seed of the Word of God?

    e. Read 1 Corinthians 3:5-8. What is the principle of sowing, watering and reaping?

2. How did the following respond to Jesus Christ at His birth?

    a. Mary (Luke 1:26-38,46-55; 2:19,33)

    b. Joseph (Matthew 1:18-25; Luke 2:33)

    c. The shepherds (Luke 2:8-20)

    d. The Magi/wise men (Matthew 2:1-12)

    e. The innkeeper (Luke 2:1-7)

    f. Herod (Matthew 2:1-8,16)

    g. Simeon (Luke 2:22-35)

    h. Anna (Luke 2:36-38)

3. Write the names of specific people you know who would respond like any of the above next to those names above.

Note the principle of sowing, watering and reaping in 1 Corinthians 3:5-8:

- Growth is a process. It takes time.
- It is a partnership. It requires working together with other people and processes.
- Productivity is the result. It is only God that can bless with fruitfulness.

Illustration: Whose Agenda—Yours or God's?

Recently I met a spiritually hungry young woman who was attending a California university. She came to church several times with our family. She tried on several occasions to attend a Bible study group sponsored by a national Christian organization on her own campus. She was frustrated by the fact that every time she asked questions about the Bible and who God is, the Christians in the group became defensive. It was clear to her that even though she was searching and seeking, many Christians had their own agenda. They did not want to be moved to a level of discomfort within the context of a Bible study or prayer meeting to answer the questions of a seeker.

Such incidents are repeated hundreds of times throughout the country. The Church needs to move from a posture in which it feels it must defend the faith back to an emphasis on personal witnessing.

1. What are some difficult questions you have heard people ask about God, Jesus or the Bible?

2. What do you do when someone begins to ask difficult spiritual questions in a group situation?

3. Think back to the time before you became a believer. What are some tough questions you wanted to ask?

   Did you ask them? If so, what were the responses of those of whom you asked?

Session 4

The Misconceptions

Understanding and Addressing Popular Beliefs
Part I

Introduction

Over the past generation America has undergone a significant cultural shift from being at least a nominally Christian culture to becoming a "post-Christian" culture. Yet Christians continue to use the evangelistic methods and models used successfully by previous generations as if nothing has changed. The result has been 10 to 15 years of declining numbers of people responding to Christ. This lack of response can be very disheartening for enthusiastic Christian witnesses, but it does not have to be that way.

Christians today, just as they have always been, are challenged to have an understanding of our times. Just as Jesus tailored His message to the Samaritan woman at the well (see John 4:4-42) and Paul geared his message to a pluralistic audience (see Acts 17:16-34), we are to "become all things to all men," to understand the culture and the times, so that in the process we may win some to salvation in the Lord Jesus Christ (see 1 Corinthians 9:22).

Evangelistic models, methods and apologetics—the defense of Christian faith—can sometimes get in the way of presenting the gospel truth. We must remember that these are a means to an end. We are not called to win arguments but to win people who are trapped in spiritual darkness—people who need the light of the Lord Jesus Christ (see Acts 26:18).

Objective

In this session we will discuss Satan's deception strategy against spiritual seekers as well as the key deceptions behind the classical world and contemporary religions and the cults. This is part I of two sessions that will cover twelve popular beliefs opposing the gospel that are held by many Americans and how to address seekers who hold these belief systems.

Key Verse

"But you shall receive power when the Holy Spirit has come upon you; and you shall be witnesses to Me in Jerusalem, and in all Judea and Samaria, and to the end of the earth." Acts 1:8

Preparation

Pray

- Ask God to keep you alert and reveal any areas where Satan may have a foothold in your own life so that you can deal with them accordingly (see Ephesians 4:27).
- Ask God to help the class members discern the traps of the devil so that with the Lord's help they can avoid them (see 2 Corinthians 2:11).
- Ask God to help you as a group to enlighten others about how the devil works and what the truth about God really is and what He has to offer them (see 2 Corinthians 4:4).

Prepare

- ❑ Read through the material thoroughly.
- ❑ Based on your personal reflection and the knowledge of who will attend the class, anticipate questions that they might ask and how you might answer them scripturally.
- ❑ Think through all items in this session—questions for consideration or discussion to help you guide the class in the right direction and avoid sidetracks and fruitless discussion.
- ❑ For session 4A: Make overhead transparencies of "The Faces of Deception" chart (pp. 82-83) or make photocopies of the chart as a handout for each student.
- ❑ For session 4B: Photocopy **Option:** "Illustration: A Legacy of Love" (p. 84).
- ❑ Provide Bibles, paper, pens or pencils for those who might need them.
- ❑ Make a copy of "The Misconceptions: Understanding and Addressing Popular Beliefs—Part I: Take Action" (pp. 80-81) for each group member.

Practice

At the end of each session is a Take Action plan. Use it to summarize the session, go over the action plan with students and encourage them to follow through on the action. As the leader of the study, you are strongly encouraged to practice what is learned so that you can share from your experiences—both the successes and failures—to help stimulate discussion and edify the class, as well as set an example for them to follow.

Important note before you begin this session: If you plan on completing this session in only one 60-minute class meeting, skip session 4A and go directly to 4B "Popular Beliefs in America Today—Part I" beginning on page 72.

Session 4A

Introduce the Session (10 Minutes)

✝ Pray that this session will open the eyes of group members to the many spiritual deceptions that abound in our culture and that they will learn to discern God's truth.

➻ Welcome the class members. Ask members to share things they have heard or read in the news that reflect the spiritual deception that is rampant in our culture.

➻ Ask one or two volunteers to share their written personal testimonies.

Step 1: The Deception of the Tolerance Agenda (5 Minutes)

➻ Introduce the topic by explaining:

It seems that the only moral absolute in our culture is "tolerance!" We are to be tolerant of everyone and everything so long as "nobody gets hurt." We are especially never to say anything negative or contradictory in the areas of religion or lifestyles. With the culture taking such an authoritative stance against any kind of exclusivism—whether it is the first commandment or the gospel—there is enormous pressure on Christians to soft-pedal the mandate to reach the lost. It is so easy to cave in to that pressure and compromise God's call to us to personally witness to others.

The underlying goal of those who cry out for tolerance in the area of religion is not easy to miss. The aim is not just an attempt to establish the rights of every individual to select a religion of his or her choice; rather it is a calculated and imperialistic attempt to bully us into agreeing that all religions are equally valid. As we will see in this lesson and the rest of this course, the claim that all religions are equally valid in meeting the needs of humanity is impossible: historically, biblically or spiritually.

Option: Crafty Satan Is the Founder of Deception (10-15 Minutes)

- Read Genesis 3:1-13 to the whole group.
- Ask class members to brainstorm the various aspects of Satan's deception as you write their responses on an overhead transparency, white board, chalkboard or newsprint. Be sure the following aspects are included.

1. Satan is crafty and attractive in the way he presents sin (see v. 1).
2. He questions God (see v. 1).
3. He suggests that there is illumination apart from the God of the Bible (see v. 5).
4. He presents the thought that illumination could come to Adam and Eve by disobedience to God's laws (see vv. 1,5).
5. He suggests that they will not die as a result of eating the fruit and falling into sin. This suggestion opens the door to other possibilities following death, including that of reincarnation (see v. 4).
6. He promises that if they eat of the fruit, they shall be like God (see v. 5).
7. He questions God's real intentions and suggests that their personal rights have been violated by God (see vv. 1,5).
8. He mysteriously disappears once his temptation has succeeded in bringing about the spiritual fall of Adam and Eve.
9. He creates a definite alienation between God and His creation, Adam and Eve (see vv. 7-13).

- Explain:

The Bible recognizes Satan as a created angel, inferior to God, who foolishly turned away from God and became God's enemy. Satan plants the seeds of rebellion, disillusionment and ignorance of the real facts concerning God and His plan for humanity.

- Assign the following Scripture verses to various group members. Give them a moment to read their passages.

Mark 1:13	1 Peter 5:8	Revelation 12:9
John 8:44	1 John 2:16	Revelation 20:2
1 Corinthians 7:5	1 John 3:8	Revelation 20:10
2 Thessalonians 2:8,9	2 John 1:7	

- Ask each one to share what his or her passage says about Satan.
- List their responses on the board or overhead.
- Read James 1:13-15 aloud, then explain the following:

Sin is the result of giving in to Satan's temptations and believing his lies.

- Ask a few group members to briefly share at least one spiritual deception Satan has brought across their paths that they have discerned as temptation and have overcome with the help of God.

Step 2: The Faces of Deception (45-50 Minutes)

At the risk of oversimplification, the purpose of this section is merely to list some of the distinctive spiritual beliefs from the ancient world religions, from the contemporary religious scene and from cults.

- Put the transparency of "The Faces of Deception" chart on the overhead projector or give handouts to students. Point out how Christianity is unique and distinct from all other systems of belief.
- Divide students into seven groups.
- Assign one of the common assumptions listed below to each group. Ask them to discuss the assigned assumption, then write a response to that assumption.
- When the groups are finished, ask one representative from each group to share the assumption and the response they have written.

The false assumptions are:

1. All religions are basically the same.
2. All religious leaders are basically the same.
3. All religions teach basically the same things.
4. All religions view human problems in basically the same way.
5. All religions explain human suffering in the same way.
6. All religions have basically the same spiritual goals for which to strive.
7. All religions teach basically the same source of moral truth.

Two-Meeting Track: If you want to spread this session over two meetings, stop here and close in prayer now. Inform students of the content to be covered in your next meeting.

Session 4B

Preparation

Pray

- ✝ Ask God to help you quickly spot false doctrine as you talk to unbelievers so that you might address it.
- ✝ Ask God to remind you how you have seen these false doctrines at work in our culture recently.
- ✝ Ask God for a class of students open to learning new approaches to unbelievers who are trapped in deception.
- ✝ Ask God for several opportunities for those in your group to address people trapped in false doctrine so that there can be shared experiences and learning together to be more effective witnesses.

Prepare

- ❑ Photocopy **Option:** "Illustration: A Legacy of Love" (p. 84) for each student.
- ❑ Provide Bibles, paper, pens or pencils for those who might need them.

Introduce the Session (10 Minutes)

- ➧ Begin the session with prayer.
- ➧ Ask volunteers to share how they have seen some of the common belief systems that were covered in the last session at work during the past week.

Step 3: Popular Beliefs in America Today—Part I (45-50 Minutes)

> **Special note:** There is a lot of information to cover in this session. You will have to use your best judgment to choose how much to present to your group.

- ➧ Be sure students have paper and pens or pencils for taking notes.
- ➧ Discuss the following information with the whole group. If there is time after sharing the information, divide members into small groups and assign each group one of the six beliefs for which they will come up with questions and comments to make to someone who holds that belief.

1. **All religions are the same.**
   Do you think it is possible to disagree with the statement "all religions are the same" and at the same time respect any individual's right to choose the religion that he or she prefers? Are "disagreement" and "intolerance" the same thing?

Key Scriptures

"There is one God and one Mediator between God and men, the Man Christ Jesus" (1 Timothy 2:5).

"Jesus said…'I am the way, the truth, and the life. No one comes to the Father except through me' " (John 14:6).

Bridge Statements and Questions

Use the following information to develop inroads for discussing with someone who holds this belief:

- No religion teaches that all religions are the same. Even Hinduism, which claims to be the most tolerant religion, is intolerant toward religions such as Christianity and Islam because they claim to be "the" way to God.
- If all religions are the same, that would make them equally valid. But since they are in fact different, they yield different results and thus they cannot all be equal.

Questions to ask an unbeliever: "Have you ever investigated the uniqueness of Jesus Christ? Would you mind if I took a few minutes of your time to share pertinent information on this subject? I would like your response to some of the differences I see between Christianity and what you believe."

It is important to clearly establish what makes Christianity totally different from other world religions:

a. Christianity exclusively offers a personal relationship with God that is unique. Vital to Christian belief is the fact that God wants to share His life and love with every human being. Although He is a holy God, He is not out of reach of any human being. He has expressed Himself through Jesus Christ, His Son. He has paid the ultimate price for our sins because of His great love for His creation.
b. Although Christianity is not the only religion that acknowledges the problem of human sin and suffering, it is the only religion that provides a way for human beings to be delivered, cleansed and preserved from sin.
c. Having a *living* Savior makes Christianity unique. In Hinduism, many leaders have claimed to be "God," but they are all dead or will soon die. Buddha more modestly claimed only to know the way to "enlightenment," but he also died. Mohammed claimed to speak for God, but he died as well. Of all the great religious leaders of the world only one, Jesus Christ, rose from the dead. His tomb alone

remains empty. Over 500 eyewitnesses at one time saw Him in His resurrected state right here on this earth (see 1 Corinthians 15:6). These truths set Christianity apart.

2. **I believe in selecting the best from every religion and coming up with my own system of belief.**

Issues for Discussion

One must clearly recognize the dangers of self-made belief systems.

- When you are drawing from all kinds of religious traditions, both good and evil, light and dark, true and false, it is important to realize that many of these religions are in serious conflict with each other.
- Many self-made syncretistic belief systems involve occult experiences and practices that draw the seeker away from the God of the Bible and from the truth and the light. These practices will cause you to think that everything is relative. However, no reasonable and workable answers are offered by self-made religion to problems such as sin, disease, death and suffering. True forgiveness and redemption is only provided by Jesus Christ.

Key Scripture

I am the door and anyone that comes to God any other way is a thief and a robber (paraphrased from John 10:1,7-9).

Bridge Statements and Questions

How does one objectively establish that the belief system she or he has selected is, in fact, the best from every religion? Is there an objective way to determine if the belief system that a person who syncretizes—selecting beliefs from various religions—has, in fact, selected a system that will in fact work for him or her?

3. **Atheism says that there is no God. Agnosticism says that you can't know whether or not there is a God.**

Issues for Discussion

To be an atheist or an agnostic, one must also be a skeptic. Atheists and agnostics have usually been soured by bad experiences with Christianity or another religion so they have developed a sense of rebellion against any established religion. Scripture establishes that without faith it is impossible to please God; one must first believe that God exists and that He rewards those that diligently seek Him (see Hebrews 11:6).

Many people do not believe in God because they really do not know Him. Paul talked about this in Acts 17 when he reminded the Athenians that they worshiped the unknown God (see vv. 22-31). Paul emphasized that it was this God that created the world and everything in it. He gives us life and breath; He gives us the power to live and to move. He is not the result, or the figment, of human imagination. One day He will judge all people. God has expressed Himself through nature. He has written His law upon every human heart (see Romans 2:14,15). He has sent His Holy Spirit to convict the world of sin, righteousness and judgment (see John 16:8-11). He is open to the cry of every human heart that seeks after Him and He desires to communicate with each one of us.

Key Scripture
"The fool has said in his heart, 'There is no God' " (Psalm 14:1).
"Gentiles...show that the requirements of the law are written on their hearts" (Romans 2:14,15, *NIV*).

Bridge Statements and Questions
If there is no God, then where did we come from? Living without God leaves us with a sense of disconnectedness. There is greater factual evidence to establish that God exists than there is to establish that He does not. Research will, in fact, confirm that it will take more faith to believe that God doesn't exist than to believe that He does exist.

4. Evolution gives us the best explanation of how our world was created.

Issues for Discussion
In 1859 Charles Darwin stated his theory of evolution in his book *The Origin of Species*. This theory implied that all living species, including human beings, evolved from lower life forms over millions of years. He made the case that in a competitive, changing environment "only the fittest survive" and that the "natural selection" (and the elimination) of species occur when living organisms pass on (or are unable to pass on) their genes to future generations.

At first, most of the best Christian scientists and theologians adjusted to Darwin's theory with the belief that God could have used evolution as a means to achieve the design He wanted. But naturalistic scientists and others began to claim that the process of evolution was capable of explaining all present life forms. Some even claim that the natural, material world is all there is.

Many evolutionists began to attack the biblical account of creation because it is contradictory to the theory of evolution. This has led to over a century of sometimes acrimonious debate between those who deny divine design (naturalistic evolutionists) and those who defend it (creationists, including both those who believe in an "old earth" and those who believe in a relatively "new earth").

The interesting thing is that both Christian and non-Christian scientists today are increasingly rejecting the dogmatic denial of divine creation. The theory of evolution is plagued with many inconsistencies and contradictions of the fundamental laws of science and nature. It is clear that in many ways it is much tougher to believe in evolution than in Creation.

An interesting twist on the theory of naturalistic evolutionism is the New Age teaching that the next great leap in evolution is going to be a "spiritual" one. What this means is that humanity will evolve into a higher state of spiritual consciousness and being. Not coincidentally, this was the precise suggestion that Satan made to Adam and Eve—they would become as God once they ate the forbidden fruit (see Genesis 3:5). (**Note:** There are numerous books and excellent resources on the subject; some of them are listed at the end of this session's leader's notes on page 79 as well as in appendix C).[1]

Key Scriptures

"In the beginning God created the heavens and the earth" (Genesis 1:1).

"In the beginning was the Word, and the Word was with God, and the Word was God. He was in the beginning with God. All things were made through Him, and without Him nothing was made that was made" (John 1:1-3).

Bridge Statements and Questions

In a world of complexity and beauty, would it not make sense to believe that things just did not happen by chance? Who do you say created the first living organism? (Or: How was the first living organism created?) If all of us are here only as a result of chance, then can there be any compelling reason or meaning for your life?

5. **God is in you and you are God.**

This religious belief, which is derived from eastern pantheism, has been popularized in recent years by many celebrities such as Shirley MacLaine. Although humanists do not claim to be religious, they center their search for the answers to life within themselves and their humanness. The belief that the ultimate answers in life are to be found "within you" has provided the energy and financial impetus to the self-help and self-improvement movements. This belief encourages people to discover God in their own way, often through various meditative and occult practices.

Issues for Discussion

The Bible clearly states that God and His creation are separate (see Genesis 1:1; Romans 1:20). If we were God, or evolving to be God, certainly there would be no reason for Jesus Christ to come in human form and die a sacrificial death on the cross to provide for human salvation. Scripture says that God made human beings "in His image" (Genesis 1:26,27) and a little lower than the angels (see Psalm 8:4,5; cf. Hebrews 2:6,7). However, the Bible also clearly teaches that we all have turned away from God (see Isaiah 53:4-6). Therefore it is vain to believe that divinity is within you apart from the cross of Christ and repentance from sin. What is within a person not surrendered to Christ is a human heart "desperately wicked" and in need of salvation (see Jeremiah 17:9). Any human being who considers him- or herself as divine is totally deceived.

None of those who have claimed to be divine have escaped the travesties of human sin, suffering and disease. To press a claim of divinity and be subject to any sin, suffering or disease is a claim of gross self-deception. In one of his lectures at Oxford, C. S. Lewis stated that when man is enraptured with himself, he will eventually end up worshiping the devil. This is confirmed when one observes how religion steeped in the worship of creation (either the natural world, the objects in the natural world or the human self) often involves occult practices. Therefore, self-worship, resulting in an unsatisfied desire for supernatural power, will ultimately lead us either to the foot of the throne of the almighty God (if we repent) or to Satan himself.

In order to help people realize that they are God (i.e., to come into a higher state of consciousness), eastern religions and New Age cults use occult practices. These secret or hidden practices open one's mind, heart and spirit to the powers of hell and darkness, not to the powers of light and truth of the God of the Bible. If we could become God, that would certainly be something to boast about! But the Bible strongly declares that salvation is not in yourself or your own divinity; rather it is only by God's grace, a gift of God, not of works "lest anyone should boast!" (see Ephesians 2:8,9). There is absolutely nothing we can do to become God. We are created human beings. But because He loves us, if we recognize Him for who He is and accept the expression of salvation through Jesus Christ, we will come to know Him in a personal and powerful way.

Key Scriptures

"God created man in His own image; in the image of God He created him; male and female He created them" (Genesis 1:27).

"What is man that You are mindful of him....For You have made him a little lower than the angels" (Psalm 8:4,5).

6. Death is not followed by heaven or hell.

Issues for Discussion

Millions of westerners believe in reincarnation, a foundational belief of Hinduism and Buddhism, which says that at death a person's soul has the ability to come again to earth and inhabit a new body, recycling as many times as needed to reach the goal of becoming a divine being at one with the ultimate—translated as *moksha* and *nirvana*. In this understanding, one's situation in the this life is determined, or fated, by one's *karma*—the totality of one's actions and thoughts—in the last life, and one's station in the next life is determined by one's *karma* in this life. The concepts of *karma* and reincarnation have also been taught in Greek and Roman religions (with different terminology), in variant forms of mystical Judaism, and in occult and New Age religions.

The twin doctrines of *karma* and reincarnation avoid the biblical teaching on heaven and hell: "It is appointed for men to die once, but after this the judgment" (Hebrews 9:27). They suggest that as our souls evolve to higher planes of consciousness, we become one with the universe, or cosmos. These doctrines also facilitate the doctrine of universal salvation—according to *karma* and reincarnation every human soul is being processed through numerous bodies and eventually, having achieved the state of perfection, will become God.

Key Scripture

"It is appointed for men to die once, but after this the judgment" (Hebrews 9:27).

Bridge Statements and Questions

Is death the absolute end? No matter what one's religious outlook, the observation that life ends with the nothingness of death is very disturbing. Death mocks our hopes, dreams, aspirations, talents and hope for meaning. It is a tragic end to a human life that has been filled with God's divine power and supernatural touch.

People who believe that death is the absolute end take an awful risk of being unprepared to meet God. When they arrive before the judgment throne of God, their sins and rebelliousness will condemn them to hell. However, while they are alive there is still time to consider God's claim on their lives. If they would just investigate the biblical view of life after death, they might be better prepared to face the God who created them—the eternal Judge.

Does reincarnation give the hope that we really need in the face of death? In the face of death the belief in reincarnation gives scant comfort. It is a cycle with no hope and no end. It is based upon a strict doctrine of works. It is also based upon the flimsy and fraudulent claims of those who ask us to believe in their supposedly remembered past lives.

Belief in *karma* and reincarnation gives a person the false hope that there will be opportunities after death to find salvation and removes the necessity and urgency to repent from one's sins and to bow to Jesus Christ who provided sacrificially for *my* sin.

There is also the assumption of self-salvation, based on a system of personal effort and works. But Scripture is clear that all of us have gone astray as human beings (see Isaiah 53:6; Romans 3:23) and that none of us can save ourselves. Reincarnation can offer *no* forgiveness, *no* repentance, *no* hope and *no* eternal life with your Creator; it only offers eternal recycling until you are at one with the universe, i.e., yourself.

What is the biblical answer to death? We have a choice: we can believe that death is an absolute dead end, an endless dead end, or not a dead end at all but an ushering into the presense of the holy God. Jesus Christ made the following astounding claims (based upon John 5:21-30):

a. God has given Jesus authority to eternally judge every person (vv. 22,27);
b. The dead will be raised to eternal life at the sound of His voice (vv. 21,25,28);
c. Those who have "done good" Jesus will rise to eternal life (v. 29);
d. Those who have "done evil" will be condemned (v. 29).

Our only hope is to believe in Him who ultimately has the power and authority to raise us from death into everlasting life.

Option: Illustration: A Legacy of Love (10-15 Minutes)

- Give each group member a copy of the illustration.
- Read and discuss the illustration with the whole group. **Or:** Divide students into groups of four or five and have them discuss the questions in small groups.

Take Action

- Give each member a copy of the Take Action page. Discuss with the whole group. Encourage them to take the actions suggested.

Note:

1. The following books are recommended resources on evolution:
Michel J. Behe, *Darwin's Black Box* (New York: Free Press, 1996).
Philip E. Johnson, *Darwin on Trial* (Downers Grove, Ill.: InterVarsityPress, 1993).
Philip E. Johnson, *Defeating Darwinism* (Downers Grove, Ill.: InterVarsityPress, 1997).
Hugh Ross, *The Creator and the Cosmos: How the Greatest Scientific Discoveries of the Century Reveal* God (Colorado Springs: NavPress, 1993).

Understanding and Addressing Popular Beliefs Part I

Take Action

Session Summary

- Religious tolerance must not be confused with forcing people to agree that all religions are equally valid. Religious tolerance does mean respecting other people's rights to believe as they choose.
- The founder of deception is Satan himself and in Genesis 3:1,4,5 he tells his lies which continue to be perpetrated to this day.
- The faces of deception are many. Spiritual deception continues to thrive through the spread of classical world religions, contemporary religions and cults. It is easy to see how the lies that were sown as seeds in Genesis 3:1,4,5 continue to abound to this day.

In this section, we have looked at six belief systems and the scriptural answers to them. We have also provided insights into how a Christian might approach people who believe such doctrines.

Action Plan for the Week

1. Memorize Acts 1:8 by writing it on a 3x5-inch index card and post it in a prominent place where you can read it often.

2. Strike up a conversation this week with a non-Christian to determine what he or she believes about God and see if you can address, both scripturally and in love, the claims of Jesus Christ to that person.

3. Continue to pray for the unbelivers on your prayer list. Ask God for opportunities to share your life with at least one person on the list.

Closing Prayer

Thank you, Father, for shedding Your light to dispel the dark deception planted by the devil himself and perpetrated throughout human history. Thank You for shedding light on my own life, helping me find the way. I pray that You will give me a sense of understanding, empathy and love toward those who still wander in spiritual darkness. Help me to lovingly confront false belief systems and share the truth with those who are enslaved by them. I recognize that there is salvation in no other name under heaven but in the name of the Lord Jesus Christ. Please allow me the privilege, even this week, of sharing that good news with others. In Jesus' name, I pray. Amen.

The Faces of Deception

	The Beliefs	Ancient World Religions						
		Classical Greek & Roman	Mainstream Hinduism & Mahayana Buddhism	Thereveda Buddhism & Taoism	Animism	Gnostic, Nature & Mystery Religions	Islam	Occult and Spiritism
NON-CHRISTIAN BELIEFS	Many gods, goddesses, spirits and demons	yes	yes	irrelevant	yes	yes	no	yes
	Appeasing, manipulating or bartering with the spirit world	yes	yes	irrelevant	yes	yes	no	yes
	Continuing blood sacrifice and other rituals	yes	yes	irrelevant	yes	yes	yes	yes
	Mythological, nonhistorical legends	yes	yes	irrelevant	yes	yes	yes	yes
	Secret knowledge only for elite "knowers"	yes	yes	irrelevant	yes	yes	no	yes
	Magic arts, spells, hexes, taboos, astrology	no	yes	irrelevant	yes	possibly	no	yes
	Confusion of identity between creator and created; the self is God or part of God (pantheism and panentheism)	no	yes	yes	possibly	yes	no	yes
	Ethics/morals derived from humans (or self); no absolutes; everything is relative	no	yes	no	no	yes	no	yes
	Reincarnation	yes	yes	yes	possibly	yes	no	yes
	Contacting the dead	yes	yes	no	yes	yes	no	yes
	"Salvation" by human effort	yes	yes	yes	yes	yes	yes	yes
	Pick and choose from different religions	not clear	yes	no	no	yes	no	yes
	Christ is optional, only one of several spiritual masters	NA	yes	yes	NA	yes	no	yes
CHRISTIAN BELIEFS	The One God exists eternally as three Persons: Father, Son and Holy Spirit	no	no	no	no	no	no	no
	God is infinite, yet personal; transcendent, yet immanent; God rules history	no	no	no	no	no	yes	no
	God is able to communicate clearly to people through nature and His Word	no	no	no	no	no	yes	no
	Morals are derived from divine and natural law	yes	yes	yes	yes	yes	yes	yes
	A founder with a virgin birth, a sinless life, a death that pays the sins for all humanity, raised from the dead and ascended to the right hand of Almighty God	no	no	no	no	no	no	no

The Faces of Deception

	Contemporary Religions			Cults		Scripture
	Scientism/ Denial of spirit world	New Age & Neopaganism	Folk Religions	Quasi-Christiam Cults	Psycho-logical Cults	What Holy Scripture Teaches...
NON-CHRISTIAN BELIEFS	no	yes	no	yes & no	all within	Gen.1:1; Exod. 15:11; 20:2-6; Deut. 6:4,5; Isa. 45:5,6,21,22
	no	yes	yes	yes	NA	Deut. 13:1-5; 18:9-14; 1 Kings 11:33
	no	yes	yes	yes & no	no	Matt. 26:28; Heb. 7:27; 10:10-12; 13:20; 1 Pet. 3:18
	no	yes	yes	yes	yes	1 Cor. 15:1-8,12-19; 1 Tim. 1:4; 2 Pet. 1:16
	possibly	yes	yes	yes	yes	John 1:12; 3:16; Col. 2:8-10, 16—3:1; 1 Tim. 2:4
	no	yes	yes	possibly	yes	2 Kings 17:16-18; Isa. 47:12-15; Acts 8:9-24
	no	yes	yes	yes & no	yes	1 Kings 8:27; Pss. 8:1-9; 24:1-10; 89:5-14; Isa. 40:12-17; 1 Pet. 1:24,25
	yes	yes	no	no	yes	1 Kings 8:46; Pss. 51:1-4; 143:2; Eccles. 7:20; Rom. 2:14-16; 1 John 1:5-10
	no	yes	possibly	no	sometimes	Rom. 6:23; Heb. 9:27
	no	yes	yes	no	sometimes	Deut. 18:10-12; Isa. 8:19
	yes	yes	yes	yes	yes	Gen. 15:6; Rom. 4:3; Gal. 2:15,16
	no	yes	yes	yes	yes	Exod. 20:2-5; 23:13; Josh. 1:7,8
	NA	yes	no	yes	yes	John 14:6; Acts 4:12; 1 Tim. 2:5,6
CHRISTIAN BELIEFS	no	no	no	no	no	Matt. 28:19; John 1:1-4; 14:26; 15:26; 1 Cor. 12:4-6; 2 Cor. 13:14; Eph. 4:4-6; 1 Pet. 1:2; Jude 20,21
	no	no	yes	yes & no	no	Exod. 14:21-31; 34:6-8; Pss. 2:1-12; 9:7-12; 96:1-13; Dan. 4:17,25
	no	no	yes	yes	no	Ps. 19:1-14; Rom. 1:19-23; Heb. 4:12
	no	no	yes	yes	no	Matt. 22:37-40; Phil. 4:8
	no	no	no	yes, but key points redefined	no	Matt. 1:18-23; John 1:29,30; 2 Cor. 5:21; Heb. 1:1-4; 1 Pet. 3:18

Illustration: A Legacy of Love

Before she died, Mother Teresa received secular recognition by winning the Nobel Peace Prize for working with the poorest of the poor in Calcutta, India. The religious order she founded, the Missionaries of Charity, has opened orphanages, schools, hospices and hospitals among people in the most deplorable conditions all over the globe.

For several decades Roman Catholics have been speculating about whether Mother Teresa might eventually be canonized as a saint. Perhaps because she was Roman Catholic, or perhaps because they did not understand some of the things she said, some Christians have questioned her personal faith in the Lord Jesus Christ. Yet when one examines what she has done and her personal testimony of why she did it—because of her faith in the Lord Jesus Christ—I find it difficult to doubt that she is part of God's family and in heaven with Him now.

One experience regarding Mother Teresa stands out in my mind. When I was a child, my father told me that as a labor arbitrator for the government of India he was sent to investigate the labor practices of Mother Teresa. He arrived at a time when there were not enough pillows for the poor and the needy who she housed. When he questioned her as to how she would get the pillows she needed, she was quick to share her reply.

"It's very simple. We just pray and when we pray, God sends people with pillows, or whatever else we need, to our mission. That is how we meet people's needs in Jesus' name."

Mother Teresa had profound respect for people in their spiritual search, but she recognized that salvation was only to be found through the Lord Jesus Christ. The biblical Christ is who she served and the biblical Christ is who she recommended to other seekers as part of her ministry. Jesus is the reason why she did what she did. Jesus was the one who worked through her to leave behind a legacy of saintliness.

1. What evidence in your life shows that you have a personal relationship with Jesus Christ?

2. Think of someone you know who is a living testimony of God's love. What sets that person apart from others?

3. What do you need to do to become a living testament of Jesus Christ who lives within you?

Session 5

The Misconceptions

Understanding and Addressing Popular Beliefs Part II

Introduction

This session continues to explore popular beliefs found in America today. Our purpose in examining these beliefs is twofold: (1) to reveal that spiritual deception originates in Satan's rebellion against God and (2) to unmask outworkings of this spiritual deception and rebellion in popular American beliefs.

An essential part of Christian witness is to confront the lies and expose them for what they are: feeble attempts to avoid living authentically and responsibly before Almighty God. How can we confront lies and yet avoid appearing judgmental and intolerant? It may be that no matter how sensitive we are, some people will make these kinds of accusations. This is a part of the work of evangelism (see 1 Peter 3:14; 4:14): mockery, misunderstandings and insults sometimes come with the territory.

We must never, ever be "ashamed of the gospel" (Romans 1:16). However, exposing lies does not mean that we indiscriminately "blow people away" with the truth. Rather, in the power of the Holy Spirit, God wants us to lovingly connect with people at whatever spiritual level they are, discern their needs and bring them in contact with the Lord Jesus Christ—the only One who can set any of us free from our spiritual blindness and sin.

Objective

In this session we will explore and respond to six more popular beliefs in America, identify typical popular misconceptions about Christianity and Jesus Christ, practice the admonition to "test the spirits" and begin to suggest ways that we can develop successful lifestyles of witnessing.

Key Verse

"For God has not given us a spirit of fear, but of power and of love and of a sound mind." 2 Timothy 1:7

Preparation

Pray

- ✞ Ask God to help you discern false doctrine as you talk to unbelievers so you can address it.
- ✞ Ask God for students open to learning new approaches to unbelievers trapped in deception.
- ✞ Ask God for several opportunities for those in your group to address people trapped in false doctrine, so there can be shared experiences and learning together to be more effective witnesses.

Prepare

- ❑ Read through the material thoroughly.
- ❑ Based on your personal reflection and the knowledge of who will attend the class, anticipate questions that they might ask and how you might answer them scripturally.
- ❑ Think through all items in this session—questions for consideration or discussion to help you guide the class in the right direction and avoid sidetracks and fruitless discussion.
- ❑ For Session 5B: Photocopy "Testing the Spirits" (p. 101); "The Witnessing Conversation" (p. 102) and **Option:** "Illustration: A Divine Appointment" (p. 103).
- ❑ Provide Bibles, paper, pens or pencils for those who might need them.
- ❑ Make a copy of "Session Five: Take Action" (p. 99) for each group member.

Practice

At the end of each session is a Take Action plan. Use it to summarize the session, go over the action plan with students and encourage them to follow through on the action plan. As the leader of the study, you are strongly encouraged to practice what is learned so that you can share from your experiences—both the successes and failures—to help stimulate discussion and edify the class, as well as set an example for them to follow.

Session 5A

Step 1: Popular Beliefs in America—Part II (45-50 Minutes)

Special note: There is a lot of information to cover in this session. You will have to use your best judgment to choose how much to present to your group.

- Be sure students have paper and pens or pencils for taking notes.
- Review the six popular beliefs in America that were discussed in the last session and explain that in this session you will discuss the six remaining of the twelve popular beliefs.
- Continue by discussing points 7 through 12.
- Discuss the following information with the whole group. If there is time after sharing the information, divide members into small groups and assign each group one of the six beliefs for which they will come up with questions and comments to make to someone who holds that belief.

7. I can be a Christian without belonging to a church.

Explanation

It is clear that the person who says this has had a bad experience with church somewhere along the line. It is important to avoid being defensive about the Church.

The fact is the Church is made up of human beings like you and me. In recent years, masses of people have left the Church disillusioned with what they have seen in Christians. A very important part of this disillusionment is a misunderstanding of what the Church is and what the Church is not. Let me share some facts with you about the Church of Jesus Christ.

a. The Church of Jesus Christ is not intended to be:
   - A social club with special privileges for special people. Jesus Christ came for all people.
   - A kind of militia to battle evil and take over the world. The kingdom that Jesus Christ came to bring is not of this world. It is a spiritual kingdom.
   - A corporation following the dictates of modern business management. The Church itself is to be a living organism empowered by the Holy Spirit.

➻ Before presenting the information below, ask group members to define "what church is" based on Scripture, then add the following points as needed:

b. Scripturally the Church is:
   - The Body of Jesus Christ. He is its head and the source of all wisdom (see Ephesians 5:23; James 1:5).
   - The Bride of Christ with Him as the Bridegroom. He is the source of our love and acceptance (see Ephesians 5:25; Revelation 19:7,8; 21:9).
   - A temple of the Holy Spirit, the presence of God (see 1 Corinthians 3:16). There is only one Church of Jesus Christ (see John 13:35; Ephesians 4:3,4), although there are many congregations and denominations within the larger body of the Church worldwide. All Christians are called to individual and corporate holiness.
   - A center for training, encouraging, building up and sending Christians out to bless the world (see 1 Thessalonians 5:11; 2 Timothy 2:2).
   - A haven for fellowship, regardless of the gender, age, race, religion or socioeconomic background of its members (see Galatians 3:26-28).
   - All those whom God has purchased with the blood of the Lord Jesus Christ (see Acts 20:28).

The fact is that it is possible to be a Christian without belonging to a local church, but it is not possible to live an authentic Christian life and shun the Church. The person who avoids the Church must deal with his or her disillusionment and must clear up any misunderstandings of what the Church is and what it is not. Once you have made a commitment to Christ, you need the Church and the Church body needs you in order for both to become everything that God wills and desires. When we alienate ourselves from the Church, we become the loser for it.

Key Scriptures

"Let us consider one another in order to stir up love and good works, not forsaking the assembling of ourselves together, as is the manner of some, but exhorting one another, and so much the more as you see the Day approaching" (Hebrews 10:24,25).

8. God, the earth and we are all one.

The radical environmental movement, "New Age" celebrities, the media and even children's movies are constantly telling us that all is one, everything is connected, and we are all part of a great "circle of life." Proponents of the Gaia hypothesis even suppose that mother earth itself is a living, intelligent being, greater even than the sum total of all life on the planet. While these phrases and theories may seem merely strange and harmless, behind them is a belief system totally incompatible with biblical truth.

Explanation

The study of comparative religions shows that since ancient times, humans have given the earth and nature sacred status and worshiped them. The beliefs that "all is one," "God is one," and "we are one with everything" mostly arises out of the pantheistic, everything-is-God religious traditions found in Hinduism and eastern religions as well as some Native American and other tribal beliefs. There are many variations of pantheistic beliefs ranging from Thoreau's nature-transcendentalism to the Gaia hypothesis.

The Bible clearly differentiates between the Creator and the creation. The apostle John clearly says in John 1:3,4 that the earth was created by "the Word"—later identified as Jesus Christ in verse 14—and given life by Him. Psalm 24:1 states that the earth and everything on it belongs to the Lord.

So when we worship God, we do not worship the earth and we certainly do not worship the earth as God. In Romans 1:18-32, Paul declared that people can clearly see that nature points to a powerful Creator (see v. 20). He also states that those who worship creatures rather than the Creator God are exchanging the truth for a lie (see v. 25) .

To get people to worship creation rather than the Creator has been one of Satan's greatest deceptions, even more so because it is a double deception—he causes people to worship the wrong thing which in turn causes people to believe that as they worship nature they are also worshiping God.

People who believe that God is not distinct from His creation need a relationship with a supernatural God. They are living under a terrible deception. The world and all it has to offer is God's gift to humanity, but it is clearly designed to point people to the Creator Himself, helping us see everything that He is and what He can mean to us.

Key Scripture

"For since the creation of the world God's invisible qualities—his eternal power and divine nature—have been clearly seen, being understood from what has been made, so that men are without excuse" (Romans 1:20, *NIV*).

9. **Everything is relative.**
Explanation
Relativism says there are no absolutes or moral laws. In its extreme form this belief will result in total lawlessness and chaos. Since relativists believe there are no absolutes and everything is interpreted according to the circumstances of the situation, there is a vicious cycle. Scripture is very clear that God has established His law. He gave us the Ten Commandments. In the New Testament the Ten Commandments were condensed and summarized into two (see Matthew 22:37-40).

It is also abundantly clear—with historical evidence—that when God's laws as revealed in the Ten Commandments are violated, we reap the negative results of such violation. Most people who believe in relativism, upon closer questioning, will be found to have not fully understood what relativism really means.

Relativism also releases human beings from the responsibilities of knowing right from wrong. At the seat of relativism is a sense of rebellion against the authority of God and the laws that He has put in place to sustain order in the universe. Scripture says that the Word of God is forever settled in heaven (see Psalm 119:89). Jesus said that "heaven and earth will pass away, but my words will never pass away" (Matthew 24:35).

Key Scripture
"Jesus Christ is the same yesterday, today, and forever" (Hebrews 13:8).

10. **Living a good life is the answer.**
Explanation
Many Americans believe that human beings are basically good and that if they live a relatively good life and don't hurt anybody, whichever god may be watching will overlook their minor flaws—and according to relativism there isn't any objective standard by which God is judging us anyway, so not to worry. If people are corrupt, it is due to their environment, their lack of education or the injustices in society—not because there is any fundamental spiritual problem that needs to be addressed.

However, Scripture teaches that humanity was created in God's own image (see Genesis 1:26,27); but that in turning away from God we have all been corrupted (see Genesis 3:1-8; Romans 5:12). Having been born into a sinful world, we lean toward doing wrong rather than right (see Romans 7:18-25). Nothing we can ever do by ourselves will make us good (if we could make ourselves good by our own efforts it would be occasion for boasting, which according to Romans 3:27 is "excluded." Because we are sinful and separated from God, "it was necessary" (Luke 24:46) for us to come to God through the finished work of Jesus Christ on the cross. It is God's goodness that makes us good in His sight when we trust Jesus Christ as our Savior and Lord. Trusting Christ includes acknowledging our sinfulness (see Romans 3:23), believing in Him (see John 1:12) and confessing Him as Lord (see Romans 10:9,10). In the Bible, goodness—righteousness—is dependent upon being "right with God" which leads to being right with men. Scripture is clear that apart from faith all our righteousness is as "filthy rags" to God (see Isaiah 64:6). It is only when by faith we die to our natural selfishness and live in the power of the Holy Spirit that we can experience true freedom from guilt and become good in God's sight (see Romans 8:1-4).

Key Scriptures

"For all have sinned and fall short of the glory of God" (Romans 3:23).

"Therefore, just as through one man sin entered the world, and death through sin, and thus death spread to all men, because all sinned" (Romans 5:12).

11. God contains both good and evil or God is beyond good and evil.

Explanation

Many people believe in a god similar to "the Force" in the *Star Wars* movie trilogy. According to these films there is a battle between good and evil in which the hero must learn to use the Force to win the battle. But he must be very careful because while the good side of the Force can help him, the dark side of the Force has the potential to corrupt him.

The belief that God incorporates both good and evil is rooted in pagan religions and other Eastern mystical religions. Hinduism, for example, includes good gods, evil gods and gods that are both good and evil. Buddhist meditation seeks to free the mind from the mental categories of good and evil. Occultists believe there is black and white magic, and evil and good witches.

The attempt to break down the distinction between good and evil is an old trick of Satan. If he can get people to believe that there is evil in God, then in their minds there might not be such a big difference between God and Satan. Maybe then he can even convince them that his personality, manifestations or lies—as evil as they are—are good.

Scripture is very clear that God is perfect and good. God is light and life (see John 1:4). In Him there is no darkness at all (see 1 John 1:5). Scripture says the God of the Bible is good (see Psalm 145:9) and He is holy (see Isaiah 6:3). He is almighty (see Genesis 17:1) and all powerful (see Isaiah 50:2). Satan is the enemy of God and his forces are evil (see 1 John 3:8). There is no middle road between good and evil; there is no way to avoid having to make a choice between two distinct alternatives. The human heart is a battlefield between good and evil, between God and Satan. And the Bible is clear that light cannot fellowship with darkness (see 2 Corinthians 6:14; 1 John 1:5-7).

Key Scriptures

"For the LORD is good; His mercy is everlasting, and His truth endures to all generations" (Psalm 100:5).

12. Hope for the future of our planet lies in global unity

Explanation

Globalism is the idea that each country should lose its national identity in favor of coming together as a one-world family. According to this viewpoint, there is either no more need for religion or all the distinctive doctrines of religions must be disregarded in an attempt to achieve a new global family.

The idea of a hope for a unified human race is nothing new. We encounter the concept very early in the Bible with the incident at the Tower of Babel (see Genesis 11:1-9). Throughout history rulers have come and gone who have tried to unify their worlds. We can expect to see similar attempts in the future and on until the end of time. In fact, the book of Revelation describes a global unity in the future that is spearheaded by the Antichrist and is inspired by Satan himself (see Revelation 13). This counterfeit global unity is followed by catastrophic events in the earth (see Revelation 14—18), the final destruction of Satan and his allies (see Revelation 19—20) and the establishment of Christ's "a new heaven and a new earth" (Revelation 21—22).

However, there is already a truly global family of believers that God is gathering, the Church of Jesus Christ, among whom are represented redeemed people from "every tribe and tongue and people and nation" (Revelation 5:9). Christ intends the gospel to be preached throughout the whole world. When believers from different tribes, languages and cultures recognize that they have all been bought with the same blood, it causes injustices to be addressed, animosities to be forgiven, prejudices to be renounced and reconciliation to flow like a river.

Key Scriptures

"There is one body and one Spirit, just as you were called in one hope of your calling; one Lord, one faith, one baptism; one God and Father of all, who is above all, and through all, and in you all" (Ephesians 4:4-6).

- Divide students into groups of two or three.
- Assign one of the popular beliefs to each small group, either from this session or the previous session. Instruct groups to come up with two or three bridge statements or questions and discuss how they would approach a person with that belief system.
- If there is time, have groups share their bridge statements with the whole group.

Option: Common Misconceptions About Christianity (10 Minutes)

- Explain the following information and discuss the questions with the whole group.

Having considered twelve of the most popular, but mistaken, spiritual beliefs in America, let us turn to three of the most common misunderstandings about Christianity.

- ***Christian faith and science are in conflict.*** **Archeology has continued to verify Bible stories and the biggest discoveries of science point to the God of the Bible.[1] Yet providing scientific evidence does not necessarily result in belief by the human heart. Even in Jesus' time on earth, people were looking for signs, yet even after they saw the miracles He performed, they did not believe He was the Son of God (see Matthew 12:38,39; 16:1-4).**

- Discuss:

1. **Why do you think some people refuse to believe in Christ when faced with evidence of miracles or overwhelming historical fact?**
2. **Why do others readily receive Christ?**

- ***People become Christians because they are raised in Christian homes.*** **There is no doubt that the way we are brought up will influence the way we think and believe, but it is very clear that the gospel is for all people. No matter what our background, each human has the same needs in the areas of guilt, suffering, fear of death and uncertainty about the future; needs that can only properly be addressed through the salvation that is provided in Jesus Christ our Lord. Ultimately, the issue is not how we were brought up but what decisions we will make when confronted with the claims of Jesus Christ.**

- Discuss:

1. **How has the way you were raised affected your Christian faith?**
2. **What is the reason you are a Christian?**

- *Christianity stifles personal freedom.* Quite the opposite. In John 8:34-36, Jesus said that those who continue in sin are the ones who are slaves to sin and that He came to bring spiritual freedom. Those who have their sins forgiven by confession and professing their faith in the Lord Jesus Christ have a unique peace that the Bible promises and that the world can neither give nor take away. In Romans 8:12-17, Paul suggested that even as we surrender ourselves and our will into the hand of God, He is able to grant us a unique level of freedom to love, to live and to labor for God.

➻ Discuss:

1. Define true freedom.
2. In what ways has receiving Christ liberated you?

Option: Common Misconceptions About Jesus Christ (10 Minutes)

➻ Explain the following information to the whole group.

Let's deal with some popular myths about Jesus Christ.[2]

- *Jesus Christ is just another expression of God.* The fact is that the Bible confirms that Jesus Christ was a man (see 1 Timothy 2:5; 1 John 4:2) *and* He was God in the flesh (see John 1:1-3,14). He was 100 percent God and 100 percent man. He had to be human to understand our sinfulness (see Hebrews 4:14,15). He had to be God to redeem us from that sinfulness (see 1 John 3:5).
- *Jesus Christ was only a great moral teacher.* The teachings of the Lord Jesus Christ are unique, especially in comparison to other world religions. But He is more than His teachings. He declared Himself to be the way, the truth and the life, stating flatly that no man could come to God except through Him (see John 14:6). Each human being must decide that either Jesus Christ *is* God in human flesh or that He is a liar. His teachings are powerful because they came from God Himself.
- *Jesus wasn't actually raised from the dead.* The fact is that there is abundant evidence concerning the resurrection of the Lord Jesus Christ. The chief priests had to hustle to come up with a tale when they realized that Jesus Christ had risen and His body was missing from the tomb (see Matthew 28:2,4,11-15). Over 500 eyewitnesses, over a period of approximately six weeks, saw Jesus Christ in His risen state (see 1 Corinthians 15:3-7). For 2,000 years now, people have based their hope in the risen Lord. This same risen Lord has promised that even as He rose from the

dead, those that believe in Him also will one day rise from the dead to eternal life (see John 6:40; 11:25). And for 2,000 years there has been testimony after testimony of people whose lives have been transformed by the risen Lord.

Two-Meeting Track: If you want to spread this session over two meetings, stop here and close in prayer. Inform students of the content you will be covering in your next meeting.

Session 5B

Preparation

Prayer

- Ask God to show you the wrong ways in which you might be approaching the lost around you and for the wisdom and boldness to use new approaches.
- Ask God to give you a class of students open to divine wisdom and new approaches in witnessing.
- Ask God for the results of His wisdom to become evident as the group members move into new frontiers in personal witnessing.

Prepare

- ☐ Photocopy "Testing the Spirits" (p. 101); "The Witnessing Conversation" (p. 102); and **Option:** "Illustration: A Divine Appointment" (p. 103), one for each student.
- ☐ **Option:** If possible, make an overhead transparency of "The Witnessing Conversation" (p. 102) rather than photocopies for students.

Introduce the Session (10 Minutes)

- Welcome students and begin with prayer.
- Ask one or two volunteers to share their written personal testimonies.
- Ask students to share if anyone had an opportunity to use the information from the last two sessions on the popular beliefs in America.

Step 2: Testing the Spirits (15 Minutes)

- Divide students into groups of four or five. Give each student a copy of "Testing the Spirits" and a pen or pencil. Have the small groups discuss the questions.

Step 3: Steps to Successful Witnessing (10 Minutes)

- Discuss the following points, giving personal examples where possible:
  - Be a friend.
  - Connect with the person on his or her wavelength.
  - Don't use "Christian" lingo; try to speak in their language.
  - Speak the truth in love.
  - Don't try to do the work of the Holy Spirit.
  - Don't be defensive and argue.
  - Don't use unfamiliar Scripture and translations without proper explanation.
  - Look for entry points in conversation to introduce Jesus Christ through perceived or actual needs a person may have. Use this as a stepping stone.
  - Be open to giving practical help to the person in case it is needed.
  - Avoid questions with a yes or no answer. Ask questions that will draw the seeker to express him- or herself.
  - Allow time: time to share, time to listen, time to think.
  - Use illustrations and stories when at all possible to clarify what you mean.
  - Have a personal testimony ready.
  - Be sure to be respectful of anything shared in confidence.

Step 4: The Witnessing Conversation (20 Minutes)

- Give each student a copy of the outline of "The Witnessing Conversation" and a pen or pencil.
- Display a transparency of "The Witnessing Conversation" on the overhead, if possible.
- Explain the following steps to the witnessing conversation:

1. **Identifying their spiritual journey:** Ask the person to share his or her spiritual journey. This will help you understand where he or she is coming from and how you might best approach him or her.
2. **Clarifying the spiritual journey:** Thank the person for sharing. Compliment him or her on the sincerity of his or her spiritual search. Ask for more personal details in order to engage him or her in further conversation and for better understanding.

3. **Giving accurate feedback:** You might need to say something like, "So here's my understanding of what you believe," then repeat clearly what you understand about his or her beliefs, allowing him or her to clarify your misconceptions.
4. **Sharing your personal experiences with God:** Share your own personal testimony by beginning with something like, "Like you, I too was searching. I appreciate your response to my questions and would like the opportunity to share with you what God has done in my life." Share how He has answered prayer, met needs and provided guidance in your life.
5. **Probing personal needs:** A question to ask him or her would be something like, "What are some of the problems you've had to deal with spiritually?" At this point, be prepared to address issues that have plagued non-Christians concerning Christ, the Bible, the Church and Christians. Other questions to lead into personal needs might include: "If there was a God who cared for you, what would you like Him to do for you?" "How can I pray for you?" "May I pray for you and your need right now?"
6. **Sharing the gospel:** Tell the person who Jesus is and why He came. At this point, it may be easy to follow a simple A-B-C plan:

   - **Admit** that you are a sinner—Romans 3:23.
   - **Believe** that Christ can save you—John 1:12.
   - **Confess** Christ is the Lord of your life—Romans 10:9,10.

7. **Leading in prayer:** Ask the person to follow you in a simple prayer for salvation.

Dear Father in heaven,

I come to You in Jesus' name to acknowledge my sin. I believe in what Jesus Christ has done by His death on the cross for my sins. I confess to You that I am a sinner in need of the Lord Jesus Christ. By faith I receive Him as Savior and Lord of my life. Help me, Father, to become everything You want me to be by the power that You provide through Your Word and through Your presence. Help me to become a strong Christian. In Jesus' name, I pray. Amen.

- Divide class into groups of four or five.
- Instruct the group members to brainstorm specific comments or questions they could use in each of the above seven steps.

- If there is time, have the groups share at least one good question or comment for each step with the whole class.

Option: Illustration: A Divine Appointment (15 Minutes)

- Give each group member a copy of the illustration.
- Divide class members into (or remain in) small groups. Have the small groups read and discuss the illustration and the questions that follow.

Take Action

- Give each member a copy of the Take Action page. Discuss with the whole group. Encourage them to take the actions suggested.

Notes:

1. Hugh Ross, *The Creator and the Cosmos: How the Greatest Scientific Discoveries of the Century Reveal* God (Colorado Springs: NavPress, 1995).
2. A great resource for studying this topic is Josh McDowell's *Evidence that Demands a Verdict, Volumes I and II* (Nashville, Tenn.: Thomas Nelson Inc., 1993).

Understanding and Addressing Popular Beliefs
Part II

Take Action

Session Summary

In this section we have again dealt with six popular beliefs. In addition, we have also shared some popular myths concerning Christianity and Jesus Christ. We have reaffirmed the acid test as found in 1 John 4:1-3, calling all believers to test the spirits. We have established some important preconversation guidelines. We have listed some vital components in the actual witnessing conversation. We have worked through the process of leading a person to the point of praying the prayer to receive Jesus Christ as Lord and Savior.

Action Plan for the Week

1. Memorize 2 Timothy 1:7 by writing it on a 3x5-inch index card and post it in a prominent place where you can read it often.

2. Continue to pray for those on your prayer list.

3. This week make a point of talking to several non-Christians. As soon as you pinpoint the belief system of a person, make a definite attempt to continue the conversation and witness to that person with the goal of leading him or her to the Lord Jesus Christ.

4. Ask God to bring a divine appointment your way this week—someone who needs/wants to know the Lord.

Closing Prayer

Lord Jesus,

I thank You that You are real. I thank You that You have revealed Yourself. I thank You that You are the truth in a world filled with error and deception. I thank You that You are the one who has prepared me to be a witness. I ask that You will be with me in every conversation with every non-Christian I meet. Help me to think Your thoughts and to pursue Your goals in leading the lost to knowledge of Your saving grace. I thank You that You have not given me the spirit of fear and timidity, but of power, love and of a sound mind.[1] So with great confidence I believe You for success in personal witnessing that will lead people to You and will bring honor and glory to You. In Jesus' name, I pray. Amen.

Note:

1. See 2 Timothy 1:7.

Testing the Spirits

Since the establishment of the Early Church, Christians have been faced with false teachers. Read 1 John 4:1-3 and discuss the following questions about how to grasp the differences between true and false teachers.

1. John said, "Do not believe every spirit, but test the spirits, whether they are of God; because many false prophets have gone out into the world" (v. 1). What is the relationship between false prophets and deceiving spirits?

2. Instead of naively believing everything, what are we asked to do?

3. How do we know if a spirit is from God?

One of the heresies in the Early Church seems to have been that Jesus Christ did not come in the flesh (see v. 3). John took pains in his first letter to prove that the eternal Word—whom John in 1 John 1:1 explains "was from the beginning"—was the same One the apostles experienced with their physical senses (see 1 John 1:1-3). He also warned that the antichrist spirit was in anyone who denied that Jesus was God's Son (see 1 John 2:22,23) or who denied that Jesus came in the flesh (see 1 John 4:3).

4. If someone teaches that Jesus Christ was only a man or teaches only that Jesus Christ is God, can the teaching possibly come from God? Explain your answer.

The crucial issues are:
- What does the person believe about who Jesus is?
- What does the person believe about what God has said in the Bible?
- What is his or her definition of "Christianity"? Is his or her definition consistent with the biblical truth?

The answers to these questions will serve as indicators for us to discern where people are in their spiritual lives as we witness to them.

The Witnessing Conversation

Brainstorm specific comments or questions that you could use in each of the following seven steps.

1. The spiritual journey:

2. Clarifying the spiritual journey:

3. Giving accurate feedback:

4. Sharing your personal experiences with God:

5. Probing personal needs:

6. Sharing the gospel:

    - **Admit** that you are a sinner—Romans 3:23.
    - **Believe** that Christ can save you—John 1:12.
    - **Confess** Christ is the Lord of your life—Romans 10:9,10.

7. Leading in prayer:

Illustration: A Divine Appointment

"Divine appointments" are events where God brings a Christian in contact with someone who needs the reality of the gospel of Christ in his or her life. They are *divine* because they are of God, and they are *appointments* because God in His wisdom arranges the time and place where the Christian and the non-Christian meet.

Some of these divine appointments are one-time events with strangers. More often, God gives us opportunities within our developing relationships with non-Christians friends, neighbors and relatives to share the gospel. The following is an example of an actual appointment with "divine" results:

One of the most unusual phone calls I ever received came to me while pastoring a church in a town in northern California. A young couple and their two children had been attending the church services for several months. They participated in regular church fellowship functions and spent much time in discussing their spiritual search in a nonthreatening atmosphere.

One day I received a call from the husband and father, Dale. He asked to make an appointment to see me at my office during regular office hours. What was the reason for this requested meeting? He wanted me to lead him in the prayer to receive Jesus Christ as Savior and Lord of his life. It was a joyous moment. Added to my joy was the knowledge that despite Dale's questioning mind and seeking heart, the period of open dialog we had cultivated had paid off.

It takes time to listen, time to talk and time to pray. Fruitful witnessing takes time and it pays eternal dividends, blessing people and glorifying God.

1. Have you actually led someone to Jesus Christ and prayed with him or her to receive salvation? Describe the circumstances.

2. Have you ever had a witnessing experience that seemed like a failure? Explain.

3. Have you ever had an experience that you knew was truly a divine appointment? What happened to convince you that God was influencing the circumstances to lead that person to Him?

Session 6

The Motivation

The Jesus Strategy

Introduction

Nobody is motivated to see sinners brought to salvation through the death and resurrection of Jesus Christ more than Jesus Christ Himself. He is "the Lamb of God who takes away the sin of the world" (John 1:29). He is continually and intimately in touch with human need.

Jesus was moved with compassion for the masses (see Mark 6:34). He came to the rescue of an adulterous woman as recorded in John 8:1-11. He inspired faith in the heart of a Roman official by healing his son (see John 4:46-53). He condemned the legalistic Pharisees for their insensitivity toward the seeking hearts of the Jews (see Matthew 23:2-4). He answered the questions of the outcast Samaritan woman (see John 4:1-42). He honored the request of the doubting Thomas (see John 20:24-29). He acknowledged the human needs of His own disciples (see John 21:1-14). He wept about the death of His friend Lazarus (see John 11:30-35).

Being a personal witness means bringing a person in need to Jesus Christ. It means being the light to dispel darkness (see Matthew 5:14-16). It means bringing the flavor of hope as the salt of the earth (see Matthew 5:13). It means being His ambassadors (see 2 Corinthians 5:20), bringing Christ's love and truth to humanity. It means being His servant and the servant of all (see Matthew 23:11,12).

Nothing we can do by ourselves will ever convert anyone. That is the sovereign work of God's truth and Spirit. However, we do have the high and holy privilege of being usable instruments in His hands.

Objective

This session explores the crucial aspects of the witnessing conversation with guidelines on how to lead a person to Jesus Christ. Conclusively, the imperatives of personal witnessing are highlighted. Each Christian is encouraged to launch into action, telling somebody about Jesus.

Key Verse

"Behold, now is the accepted time; behold, now is the day of salvation."
2 Corinthians 6:2

Preparation

Pray

- Ask God to help you evaluate the areas of personal discipline needed to help you be an effective witness.
- Ask God to create an atmosphere of openness as the class members pray for one another in their areas of personal weakness.
- Ask God to make you a group of overcomers so that your effectiveness in witnessing is not hampered, but enhanced.

Prepare

- ❑ Read through the material thoroughly.
- ❑ Based on your personal reflection and the knowledge of who will attend the class, anticipate questions that they might ask and how you might answer them scripturally.
- ❑ Think through all items in this session—questions for consideration or discussion to help you guide the class in the right direction and avoid sidetracks and fruitless discussion.
- ❑ For Session 6A: Photocopy the student handouts "What It Means to Be in God's Family" (p. 118) and **Option:**"Dependency on the Holy Spirit for Witnessing" (p. 119).
- ❑ For Session 6B: Make two photocopies of "Role Playing" (pp. 120-122). Cut the different situations apart making sure you have at least one for every two class members. Keep one copy for your own reference.
- ❑ Provide Bibles, paper, pens or pencils for those who might need them.
- ❑ Make a copy of "The Motivation: The Jesus Strategy: Take Action" (pp. 115-116) and "A Final Challenge" (p. 117) for each group member.

Practice

At the end of each session is a Take Action plan. Use it to summarize the session, go over the action plan with students and encourage them to follow through on the action plan. As the leader of the study, you are strongly encouraged to practice what is learned so that you can share from your experiences—both the successes and failures—to help stimulate discussion and edify the class, as well as set an example for them to follow.

Session 6A

Introduce the Session (10 Minutes)

- Welcome students and begin with prayer.
- Ask one or two volunteers to share their written personal testimonies.
- Ask volunteers to share any results they have seen from praying for people on their prayer lists.

Step 1: What Is Conversion? (10 Minutes)

- Explain the following to the whole group:

Conversion is a miracle of God.

Some expressions used to describe conversion are:

- **Being born again of the Spirit** (see John 3:5-8);
- **Becoming a new creation in Christ** (see 2 Corinthians 5:17);
- **Translated from the kingdom of darkness to the kingdom of light** (see Ephesians 5:8; Colossians 1:13; 1 Peter 2:9).

- Read Romans 10:9. Then discuss:

What must one do to be saved from sin and receive salvation?

A Transformation

- Read the following illustration aloud to the group.

A caterpillar becoming a chrysalis, then turning into a butterfly, is a picture of the conversion experience. The process of change involves one and the same person. The process of regeneration results in salvation through Jesus Christ. The convert becomes a new creation—a Christian—through the power of our Savior and Lord.

Step 2: How to Lead a Person to the Point of Conversion (20-30 Minutes)

- Provide paper and pens or pencils for those who need them.
- Assign someone to read aloud the verses in the following points.
- Explain the following information to the whole group.

Please note that there are many ways that people are converted. People have been known to accept Jesus Christ as Lord while driving a car, walking through the woods or even taking a shower. Next we will explore how to lead a person to the point of conversion. Note: List the seven main points on an overhead transparency, white board or chalkboard.

1. Make sure the person understands the scriptural meanings of:

➻ Explain the following:

- **Conversion—turning from spiritual darkness to light** (see Acts 26:18).
- **Repentance—changing your mind and purpose in life** (see Acts 3:19; 8:22).
- **Confession—agreeing with God about your sin** (see 1 John 1:8-10).
- **Acceptance of Jesus Christ as Savior and Lord** (see John 3:16).

➻ Discuss with the whole group the biblical concepts of conversion, repentance, confession and acceptance of Jesus as Savior.

2. Read key scriptures with the person.

➻ Explain the following:

Do not assume that the person understands the scripture verses. At the same time, avoid inundating him or her with too much Scripture right at the start.

➻ Ask group members to suggest a few key verses. See appendix B (pp. 125-132) for suggested key scriptures.

3. Always lead a new convert in prayer.

➻ Have them repeat a prayer after you. There is no one standard prayer, but here is a sample:

Dear Father in heaven,

I thank You for sending Jesus Christ to be my Lord and Savior. I thank You for His death upon the cross, for His resurrection and for His ascension. I acknowledge that I am a sinner. I believe that Jesus Christ died for my sins. I confess that I am a sinner and ask you to be Savior and Lord of my life. I want to put the past behind me. I want to press on to the power of the truth and the Holy Spirit of Jesus Christ. I ask You to save me from my sins and from myself. I thank You that according to Your Word, I am a new creature in Jesus Christ.[1] Help me to become the person You want me to be. Thank You for the promise of eternal life with You forever. In Jesus' name, I pray. Amen.

4. Congratulate the person on taking this first step.

5. Explain what it means to be part of God's family, God's fellowship and God's future in heaven.

Explain: **Believing in Christ means that you have been adopted into God's family and as a result you have new relationships with God and others, and you have an indestructible hope for the future. Next are some of the pictures the Bible paints for us of what it means to be in God's family.** (Use the student handout.)

➽ Give each student a copy of "What It Means to Be in God's Family." Suggest that they keep this copy in a prominent place in their homes to reflect on it from time to time.

6. After the point of conversion, lovingly instruct them on the following points:

- **Acknowledge** your newfound faith in Christ *publicly* (see Matthew 10:32; Romans 10:9,10).
- **Baptism**—follow the Lord in water baptism (see Matthew 3:13-17; Acts 2:38).
- **Confession**—as a result of living in a sinful world, you must deal with the sin that will creep into your life on a daily basis. Keep short accounts with God (see 1 John 1:8,9).
- **Devotions**—spend time every day reading the Bible and praying to the Lord (see Psalms 1; 119:9-16).
- **Evangelism**—reach out to others who do not know the Lord Jesus Christ and share your faith with them (see Matthew 28:19,20; Acts 1:8).
- **Fellowship**—join in fellowship with other Christians who can strengthen and encourage you and build you up in the faith (see Hebrews 10:25). Become involved in a local church.
- **Guidance**—be accountable to at least one other Christian and to the pastor of your local church to help keep you on track or to help you deal with personal questions or needs (see Acts 20:20; James 5:16).
- **Holy Spirit**—make sure that you pray daily and continually so that you are filled with the Holy Spirit, enabling you to live the Christian life in the strength and power of the Lord Jesus Christ, to resist temptation, to find God's grace in time of trial and to be a dynamic witness for the Lord Jesus Christ (see Romans 8:9,11,13; Ephesians 5:8)

- Discuss: **Looking back on your own life in relation to these six steps, what areas do you feel really helped you as a new Christian?**

7. Invite the person to church and begin to incorporate him or her into the body if this has not already taken place.

Option: Dependency on the Holy Spirit for Witnessing (10 Minutes)

- Have students form groups of four or five.
- Give each student a copy of "Dependency on the Holy Spirit for Witnessing" and a pen or pencil.
- Have the groups complete the matching activity and discuss the question.
- The answers are as follows:
  1. John 3:5-8
  2. Luke 11:13
  3. John 16:7-11
  4. John 16:12-14
  5. Acts 1:8
  6. 1 Corinthians 12:7-11
  7. Luke 12:11,12
  8. Ephesians 1:13,14
  9. Acts 16:6-10

Two-Meeting Track: If you want to spread this session over two meetings, stop here and close in prayer. Inform students of the content to be covered in your next meeting.

Session 6B

Preparation

Pray

- Ask God to bring to your mind lost people you know and to open doors for you to lovingly witness to them and pray for them.
- Ask God to guide the class as to who they know that needs a Christian witness and how to witness to them and pray for them.

- Ask God to fill class members continually with the Holy Spirit, so that they boldly, and lovingly make personal witnessing a part of their regular lifestyle.

Prepare

- Make two photocopies of "Role Playing" (pp. 120-122) where a variety of situations are described. Cut the different situations apart making sure you have at least one situation for every two class members. Keep the second copy for your own reference.

Introduce the Session (10 Minutes)

- Ask group members to briefly share any fruitfulness that has resulted from praying for the people on their prayer lists.

Step 3: Role Playing (20-30 Minutes)

- Pair up group members.
- Give each pair one of the role-play situations from "Role Playing."
- Have the pairs develop role plays about their given situations.
- Have each pair present their role play to the whole group.
- **Option:** If you do not have time to present role plays, ask each group to briefly share how they would begin a conversation with the person in their assigned description.

Option: The Power of Prayer Evangelism[2] (20 Minutes)

- Share the following information with group members:

During the 1990s, there has been an increasing emphasis on:

- **Prayer for revival that God will sovereignly pour out His Spirit on all the earth.**
- **Prayer for the lost to find the Savior Jesus Christ.**
- **Evangelism—actively sharing the truth in love to lead people to the Lord Jesus Christ.**

Prayer and Personal Witnessing Go Hand in Hand

- Provide paper as needed for taking notes on the following information. Explain:
  - **Start praying for the unconverted loved ones in your own family.**
  - **Prayer can shake entire nations, such as experienced by Daniel in Babylon (see Daniel's prayer in chapter 9 which is followed by extensive prophecies about the nations in chapters 10 and 11).**
  - **Prayer will send out laborers into the harvest (see Matthew 9:37,38).**

- As we are prayerfully involved in the harvest processes, we can trust God to bring in the increase.
- Pray for the work of the Spirit in the lives of the lost, to convict them of sin, righteousness and judgment (see John 16:8-11).
- Prayer can bring deliverance to those who are persecuted for their faith, such as for Peter in Acts 4:1-31; 5:17-42 and 12:1-19.
- Prayer defeats the powers of darkness (see Ephesians 6:10-18).

Prayer for Miracles Needs to Be Part of Your Witness

➻ Explain:

From the days of the Acts of the Apostles until today, miracles have been a part of God's strategy for bringing people to Himself. God is not willing that any should perish, but that all should come to repentance (see 2 Peter 3:9). Therefore, He will produce the miracles needed to draw the lost to Himself. In faith, we can expect God to hear and answer prayer and perform miracles to confirm His lordship. The greatest miracle in the universe is the conversion of a soul, translating someone from the kingdom of darkness to God's kingdom of light (see Colossians 1:13).

How to Start Witnessing Today

➻ Write the following points on the board or overhead as you explain them.

- Make a list (or add to your present list) of all the unbelievers you know in your neighborhood, at your place of employment, your relatives and other friends.
- Pray for each one on a daily basis.
- Start sharing in friendship and personal witness with them in whatever way is appropriate.

Nowhere does Scripture suggest that we present a "cheap grace" or make it easy for people to accept Jesus. It is true that Jesus has done it all; there is nothing more that we can do to be saved. However, it is important to clarify the gospel for each person so that each one fully understands what He has done and what it means to become a committed Christian. We must not emotionalize people into a decision to become a Christian.

It would be good at this point to summarize some of the key points about who Jesus is, to help give power and impetus to our witnessing. Jesus has told us:

➻ Write the following list on the board or overhead transparency as you discuss each one:

- He is the bread of life (see John 6:35).
- He is the light of the world (see John 8:12).

- **He gives you living water so that you will never thirst again (see John 4:10-14).**
- **He came that your joy might be full (see John 15:11).**
- **He came, not to condemn the world, but to save it (see John 3:17).**
- **He came to relieve your burdens and give you rest (see Matthew 11:28).**
- **Behold, He stands at the door and knocks; if you invite Him in He will come in and fellowship with you (see Revelation 3:20).**

➻ Ask a few group members to share which of the descriptions of Jesus is most meaningful to them and why.

Option: Love: The Indispensible Quality in the Jesus Style of Witnessing (10 Minutes)

➻ Read the following section on love aloud and discuss each point, assigning group members to read the scriptures, then discuss the questions at the end.

Jesus hates sin, but He loves sinners. It is not coincidental that the Gospels record no less than eight dinner invitations to Jesus. He loved to spend time with people. The target audience of His strong love were:

- **The despised—tax collectors (see Matthew 9:9-13; Luke 19:1-10)**
- **The depraved—sinners (see Matthew 9:9-13; Luke 19:1-10)**
- **The deprived—the poor (see Luke 4:18)**

1. **How can you, like Jesus, be a friend of sinners?**
2. **What do you need to change in your life and attitudes to be more of a friend to sinners?**

Note: Jesus numbered Himself among the transgressors (see Luke 22:37).

Option: Illustration: What More Can You Do? (5 Minutes)

➻ **Preparation:** Rent the video of *Schindler's List.* Forward the video to the scene near the end where the Jewish leaders are honoring Oskar Schindler, and he realizes that he is still wearing his gold ring which could have been sold and the money used to save several more people.

➻ After reading the following illustration to the whole group, have each group member find a partner and discuss the questions. Then have the pairs pray for one another and commit to keeping each other accountable to acting on what they have learned in this course.

Introduce the video clip by explaining: **Near the end of the movie *Schindler's List*, there is a very moving scene. Oskar Schindler, who had helped literally thousands of Jews escape annihilation, was now being honored by Jewish leaders. But he refused the gifts being offered to him because he felt that he had made no great sacrifice. He recognized that God had blessed him abundantly. He broke down in tears, agonizing that he could have done so much more than he did.**

- Show the video clip. Stop it when the scene is ended.
- Discuss:

1. **Why was Oskar Schindler so grieved that he could not help one more person?**
2. **What are you unwilling to give up for the sake of another person's salvation?**
3. **What more can you do than you are now doing to reach the lost with the good news of Jesus Christ?**

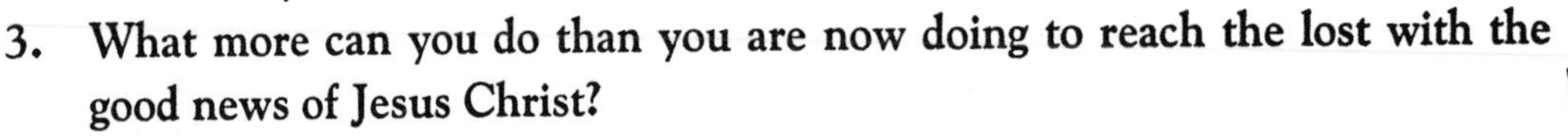

Take Action

- Give each member a copy of the Take Action page. Discuss with the whole group. Encourage them to take the actions suggested.

Step 4: A Final Challenge (5 Minutes)

- Give each group member a copy of "A Final Challenge."
- Read the challenge aloud in unison.
- Close in prayer.

Notes:

1. See 1 Corinthians 5:17.
2. Turn to the bibliography for a list of resources on prayer evangelism.

The Jesus Strategy

Take Action

Session Summary

It is apparent that we do not have much time left to be involved in the business of witnessing to people concerning who Jesus is. It is important that we clearly explain the meaning of conversion to people with whom we share. The warmth of Christ's love must shine through as we lovingly welcome new converts into the Body of the Lord Jesus Christ.

Initial instructional steps are vital to help a new Christian get started. It is important to practice with other believers and learn how to be better witnesses as we talk to a variety of people that might raise different objections to the gospel. We must never use the excuse of merely being a life witness to avoid actually having to verbally share our witness for the Lord Jesus Christ.

The power of Scripture must never be underestimated in witnessing nor overused for the new convert who is not ready to receive large doses of Scripture. There is no substitute for the dependency on the Holy Spirit to help us be effective witnesses.

The power of prayer evangelism is just now being fully explored by the Church of Jesus Christ. The best way to start witnessing is to start today. Nothing that we've ever done to this point in our lives is enough when we consider that time is short and many need to be reached before it is too late.

Action Plan for the Week

1. Memorize 2 Corinthians 6:2 by writing it on a 3x5-inch card and putting it in a prominent place where you will see it frequently.

2. Make a commitment with a partner from this group to keep one another accountable on a regular basis (meeting weekly, bimonthly or monthly) to actively witness to those around you.

3. Continue to add to your prayer list as you encounter the unsaved around you.

4. What will you specifically do this week to reach an unsaved person?

Closing Prayer

Lord Jesus Christ,

I thank You for the strategy that You have set before us. You serve as the supreme example of someone who is really concerned about the lost world. Forgive me for the times that I have lost the sense of urgency about reaching the lost. Forgive me for the times when I have tried to force people into making a decision without accommodating and being flexible to the work of the Holy Spirit. Help me to be bold and without fear to witness to all kinds of people that You bring across my path. Thank You for the power of Your Word. Help me to use it effectively. I depend entirely upon Your Holy Spirit to help me. Help me to understand, experience and explore the power of prayer evangelism in a greater way. Help me to make a fresh start in the whole area of witnessing. Help me to do more than I've ever done before in my life. I ask for Your help and blessing. In Jesus' name, amen.

A Final Challenge

Never forget that we are in a war—the battle for souls.

Never underestimate the power of prayer. God is not willing that any should perish, but that all should come to repentance.[3]

The gospel is the only hope for the world.

Every human being has free will. We need to give each person every opportunity to accept or reject the Lord Jesus Christ.

God's love in Jesus Christ is available to all people, without exception.

We are responsible to participate in the process of sowing, watering and reaping. We are not always responsible for the results of our witnessing.[4]

Time is short. One day it will be too late to witness. One day the last song will be sung, the last prayer prayed and the last message delivered. It will be time to move on to our heavenly reward. When we get to heaven, we'll have the opportunity for all eternity to worship God. We will have opportunity to grow and learn more about Him. We will also have opportunity to fellowship with all the saints for eternity. But there is one thing we cannot do in heaven. One day it will be too late to witness to the lost.

Notes:

3. See 2 Peter 3:9.
4. See 1 Corinthians 3:5-9.

What It Means to Be in God's Family

- You are no longer an enemy of God (see Romans 8:7; Ephesians 2:14-16; James 4:4); rather God is now your intimate Father (see Romans 8:15,16; Galatians 4:6).
- The Holy Spirit has given you spiritual birth (see John 3:6-8); the Holy Spirit makes His home *in* you (see Romans 8:9; Colossians 1:27) and the Holy Spirit makes you one with other believers (see 1 Corinthians 12:13; Ephesians 4:4).
- You have become a child of God (see John 1:12; Romans 8:14; Galatians 3:26; Philippians 2:15; Hebrews 12:7; 1 John 3:1,2), which means:
  a. You have become part of the great household, or extended family, of God (see Ephesians 2:19; 3:14,15).
  b. Jesus, even though He is the perfect Son of God, is not ashamed to be called your brother (see Matthew 12:50; Romans 8:29; Hebrews 2:11,12).
  c. Other believers are now your brothers and sisters in Christ (see 1 Peter 2:17; Romans 14:10).
  d. You have become part of the family that God has been building through the ages—a people from every family, tribe, tongue and nation (see Genesis 12:3; Galatians 3:8; Revelation 5:9; 7:9,10).
- As an heir in the family of faith, you have been given the rights of inheritance to the unlimited grace of God (see Galatians 3:29; 4:7; 1 Peter 3:7) and to eternal life (see Ephesians 1:11,14,18; Colossians 1:12; 1 Peter 1:4).
- You are *one* with other believers in Christ despite social and cultural differences (see Galatians 3:26,28); we are to love one another (see John 13:34,35; 1 Peter 2:17).
- You have become a member of the Church, the Bride of Christ, who is the Bridegroom (see Mark 2:19,20; 2 Corinthians 11:2; Revelation 19:7,9; 21:2,9; 22:17).
- God wants you to extend His love to others so that they may become reconciled to God and members of His family, too (see Matthew 18:12-14; 2 Corinthians 5:20; Philippians 2:9-11).

Dependency on the Holy Spirit for Witnessing

Match the following verses by drawing lines to the correct statements.

Luke 11:13	1. We are born again by the Holy Spirit, not the flesh.
Luke 12:11,12	2. The Holy Spirit is available for the asking.
John 3:5-8	3. The Holy Spirit convicts the world of sin, righteousness and judgment.
John 16:7-11	4. The Holy Spirit reveals Jesus Christ.
John 16:12-14	5. The Holy Spirit gives power for witnessing.
Acts 1:8	6. The Holy Spirit provides gifts to all believers.
Acts 16:6-10	7. When we stand before kings and governors, He gives us the right words to say.
1 Corinthians 12:7-11	8. The Holy Spirit seals new believers until the day of ultimate redemption.
Ephesians 1:13,14	9. The Holy Spirit can give you a vision of the lost who need the gospel.

In what ways has the Holy Spirit helped you in your personal witnessing experiences?

Role Playing

There is no perfect or predictable conversation when witnessing. However, it does help to role-play with other Christians to learn how to approach certain kinds of people.

How would you witness to the following?

1. Sharon works hard as a single mom with two school-age children. She had a bad experience in her marriage. She struggles to survive financially. She is always pressed for time. She makes every attempt to do the right thing. Because of her time and financial pressures and almost no Christian background, she hasn't even considered attending church. How would you approach this kind of person with the gospel message?

2. You meet a man on an airplane flight. He looks like a high-powered executive. He is a busy man. Restlessly thumbing through business magazines, he is irritated at the delay of the airplane. When you begin a conversation with him, he is short and to the point. It is clear that he is too upset to engage in small talk.

3. You work with Eddie who loves everybody and believes he is a Christian. He respects Jesus Christ whom he believes is just another god. He is into environmentalism and believes in reincarnation. He believes the earth is all one and that we are one with God. He believes that he can find God through meditation and other introspective experiences.

4. John is a church dropout in his fifties who has had bad experiences with churches. He put his faith in a pastor who stole money, committed adultery and left the church. He was on a church board where members fought among themselves. He became disillusioned and dropped out, feeling like he could still be a Christian and go to heaven without necessarily getting plugged into a church.

5. Chuck is a person who believes that success and money are what life is all about. He works hard, makes good money and feels he's a self-made individual who doesn't need God. He believes the church is only after his money and that financial success is really a sign of spirituality and maturity and worthy of admiration.

6. Ashok is an immigrant from India who owns several motels. He respects and believes in Jesus Christ although he is a Hindu. He has used his profits to build two Hindu temples already. He is taking another partner, who is also a Hindu, into his motel business with the goal of making enough profits to build at least 20 more Hindu temples in the U.S. He says he has a high respect for all Christians and likes to do business with Christians because they are honest. He is very open to entertaining and socializing with other people, including Christians.

7. Kathy is a customer relations consultant with a company that sells copy machines. She has a Roman Catholic background. She lives with a young man whom she hopes to marry someday. She is in her early 20s and doesn't feel she will live beyond the age of 40 so she wants to live her life to the fullest. She has been turned off by Christians who insist that she must accept Jesus Christ, telling her that's the only way she can know God and get to heaven. She is searching and seeking and has a difficult time trying to communicate where she is spiritually to Christians who have talked to her about accepting Jesus Christ as Lord and Savior and being born again.

8. Sally is a middle-aged woman who says, "I believe in God and go to the Catholic Church when I can. I give to the poor, am a good person and don't need to accept Jesus Christ because I am a Catholic and don't want to do anything that would make me a Protestant. My family has been Catholic for many generations. I believe that I will go to heaven when I die."

9. Ali is a 34-year-old Muslim who has his own business and is very successful. He prays three times a day. He respects all religions, including Christianity. He feels that he already believes in Jesus Christ as a great prophet and wonders why he really needs to make a commitment to Jesus Christ as Savior and Lord to go to heaven. He believes that Mohammed and Jesus are similar in many ways and that Mohammed is also a prophet of God.

10. David is a Jew who is theologically liberal. He still attends the synagogue and is a successful businessman in the community in which he lives. He respects Christians and other faiths as well. He believes that someday the Messiah will come and he's trying to follow all Ten Commandments. He really wonders why he needs to pray a sinner's prayer and accept Jesus Christ when he's obeying the Old Testament law. He believes that he will go to heaven when he dies.

11. Carl is a politician and lawyer who has run for and held several public offices. He is successful, well known and slick. He tries to be an honest person. He doesn't do anything illegal. He's on a second marriage, but he is faithfully supporting his previous wife with alimony. He says he loves his family, but he's a workaholic. He respects Christianity and other religions and believes in the right for everybody to have their own religion. He tries to be a good person, he says, and live a good life. He's never hurt anybody. He feels like we should respect all people and their right to believe whatever they want to and that people shouldn't be pushed to follow God in a specific way. Religion is a personal thing for each person and he wants to live in a country where people feel the freedom to worship and believe the way they want to, with no pressure from extreme fundamentalist Christians.

12. Ann is a college professor who has experimented with numerous religious experiences. She has a church background and has read the Bible thoroughly and can quote it. She has taught philosophy for many years and has traveled the world, visiting some of the strongholds of other classical world religions. She tries to be a good person. She is single, divorced and in her forties. She doesn't feel the need to accept the Lord Jesus Christ. She occasionally attends a liberal church and is not really connected to any vibrant church body. However, she is always open to discussing anybody's religious viewpoints. She has questions about the validity of the Bible and says that some of the biblical record is to be questioned because of new evidence that continues to emerge. She also believes that we should give credence to other prophets outside the Bible because they have something to say as well. Christians should not be so exclusive, believing in the centrality of accepting Jesus Christ in order to be saved from hell.

Appendix A

Key Bible References for Witnessing

The Problem of Human Sin

Jeremiah 17:9
John 8:34
Romans 3:23
James 1:14,15
James 2:10,11
1 John 3:8

The Provision of the Lord Jesus Christ

Isaiah 53:10-12
Matthew 1:21-23
Matthew 11:28
Luke 19:10
John 3:16,17
John 4:13,14
John 10:9-11
Acts 2:38,39
2 Timothy 1:9,10

Personal Commitment

Psalm 51:1,2
Matthew 18:3
John 3:3
John 6:28,29,47
John 11:25
Acts 3:19
Ephesians 2:1,4,5,8,9
1 John 1:8,9

Appendix B

Glossary of Terms

Agnostic—One who believes it is not possible to know with certainty that God or an afterlife exists. They are skeptical about the existence of truth, about the ability of language to convey truth and about anyone who claims to know the truth.

Animism—The belief that all natural objects and phenomena (i.e., trees, stones, the wind, etc.) are spiritual beings or inhabited by spirits.

Apologetic—A defense, explanation or justification of Christian faith in the light of specific criticisms or charges.

Astrology—The belief that one's life, love and career are influenced by the positions of the planets at birth. Based on assumed spiritual beings animating the planets and other aspects of life.

Atheist—One who has decided to disbelieve in God.

Atonement—The act that provides or makes possible salvation and reconciliation between man and God. Sinners become "at-one," or reconciled, with God through the sacrificial life and death of Jesus Christ (see Romans 3:23-25).

Buddhism—A major world religion founded by Siddhartha Gautama in the sixth century B. C. Teaches the doctrine that suffering is inseparable from existence, but that inward extinction of the self and of the senses culminates in a state of illumination called "nirvana." **Mahayana Buddhism** teaches a modified Buddhism with many gods and saviors (*bodhisattvas*). **Theravada Buddhism** adheres to original Buddhist practice, emphasizing that outside agencies (gods or spirits) are irrelevant to the religious objective of cleansing the mind (or consciousness) through meditation.

Classical Greek and Roman religions—Polytheistic (the belief in many gods) religions that believed in a moral order yet their gods and goddesses were very capricious, vain and fickle.

Confucianism—The system of morality growing out of the teachings of the Chinese philosopher Confucius (551?–479 B.C.) that teaches restraint, modesty and knowing one's exact place in the social order.

Conversion—A change in affiliation from one religion to another or the movement from non-belief in religion to belief. The Bible describes conversion as being "born again" (see John 3:8).

Convoluted—Twisted or rolled together.

Cult—An offshoot from an existing religious group, energized by a charismatic leader, extreme views, a close-knit pseudo-family that allows little or no dissent, an exclusive claim to the truth, core beliefs based on Bible passages taken out of context and often mixed with other writings (for further information on cults contact www.watchman.org).

Darkness—A metaphor for the absence of God's spiritual light, resulting in human depravity and evil (see Ephesians 5:11,12).

Denial of the spirit world refers to agnostics or atheists who effectively place all their faith in human reason and who center all their values in this material world; often they have nearly unlimited faith in science, hence **"Scientism."**

Denomination—Groups within Christianity that emphasize and feel that certain points are more important to focus on than others, yet at least in their origins agreeing on the important doctrines of the Christian truth: i.e., Assemblies of God, Baptist, Episcopal, Foursquare, Lutheran, Methodist, Pentecostal, Presbyterian, etc. are examples of only a few Christian denominations. There are over 2,500 denominations in the United States.

Divine mandate—A command to the believer from the God of the Bible and the Lord Jesus Christ.

Eternal—When referring to God, timeless, immortal with no beginning or end in terms of time. When referring to the gift of eternal life that God offers humans in Christ, it is a quality of life that extends through eternity.

Folk religions are found in all the major world religions and often includes faith healing through contacting dead holy people.

Gaia Hypothesis—The worship of "mother earth" because of the belief that we are one with nature.

Gifts and callings—Different ministry abilities and direction given by the Holy Spirit to all believers (see Romans 12:6-8).

Globalism—A term used for the coming and bringing together of the world as a whole into cooperation technologically, economically, politically and even spiritually.

Gnostics believe in intricate systems of secret truth that were only knowable by an elect, or elite, few.

Harvest—A symbolic term used by Jesus to mean bringing souls to God, just as a farmer harvests crops and brings them into his barn (see Luke 10:2; John 4:35,36).

Hindu, Hinduism—One who believes in the religious tradition of Hinduism developed over several thousand years and intertwined with the history and social system of India. There are significant variations in the beliefs that different Hindus hold, although most believe in reincarnation. There are also differences in the gods and goddesses worshiped, the scriptures used and the festivals observed. **Mainstream Hinduism** is also polytheistic; worshipers may chose among 330 *million* gods to worship. Some Hindus and some Indian religions teach **pantheism**, that all perceptions of distinctions are illusion and that all is one.

Humanists—They believe in a system, or philosophy, that human beings are of primary importance rather than God or any abstract metaphysical system. Humanism is a doctrine, attitude or way of life that rejects the supernatural and stresses an individual's dignity, worth and capacity for self-realization through reason.

Illumination—Refers to being spiritually enlightened and being filled with inner light. In Christian understanding, illumination comes from the Holy Spirit.

Islam—The word means "submission to the will of God" in Arabic and is the religion founded by Mohammed (A.D. 570–632). It is an offshoot of Judaism and Christianity. Islam is based upon the absolute unity of God, and Muslims have been taught that Christians teach three gods: God the Father, the mother Mary and their son, Jesus. Their key profession is that "there is no God but Allah and Mohammed is His prophet."

Jehovah's Witnesses—Members of the Watchtower Bible and Tract Society cult founded in 1874 by Charles Russell (A.D. 1852–1916). They deny the doctrine of the trinity, the deity of Christ and salvation by grace through faith in Christ.

Judaism—The religion that developed among the ancient Hebrews and characterized by belief in the one true God who revealed Himself to Abraham, Moses and the other Hebrew prophets and characterized by a religious life in accordance with Old Testament Scripture and the Talmud. Christianity is built on the foundation of Judaism.

Karma—The debt accumulated against the soul as a result of good or bad actions committed during one's life or lives. If a person accumulates good karma, he or she supposedly will be reincarnated to a desirable state. If a person accumulates bad karma, he or she will be reincarnated to a less desirable one.

Kingdom of God—A general reference to God's spiritual plan and purpose, as well as future government, as expressed in and through the Lord Jesus Christ. Every born again Christian is part of the kingdom of God (see Mark 1:15; 9:1; Luke 9:1,2).

Light—A biblical metaphor referring to God as the spiritual light source similar to the sun, not dependent on any other, and one who dispels all spiritual darkness (see Psalm 27:1; John 1:4,5; 8:12; 1 John 1:5). When Christians are referred to as "light," the term refers to borrowed light similar to how the moon reflects the light of the sun (see Matthew 5:14-16; 1 Peter 2:9).

Lukewarmness—Being neither hot nor cold. Spiritually speaking, it means showing hardly any interest (see Revelation 3:15,16).

Meditation—To ponder or think deeply about religious matters.

Messiah—Literally "anointed one," the deliverer long awaited by the Jews to restore the fortunes of Israel and usher in a golden age of peace and righteousness. The Greek form of the word "messiah" is *christos* or "christ." Jesus Christ is the promised Messiah (see John 1:41; 4:25,26).

Mormonism, Mormons—The common name for the belief and the members of the Church of Jesus Christ of Latter Day Saints, it is a quasi-Christian cult founded in 1830 by Joseph Smith (1805–1844). Mormons teach that Adam is the God of this world and that they can actually become gods if they follow the teachings and rituals of the Mormon Church.

Multiculturalism—A fairly recent movement toward the acceptance of many cultures on an equal basis, in which one culture is judged no better or worse than any other.

Myths, mythology—A myth is a nonhistorical story—or set of stories—that explains the origin and history of a people. The Hindu scriptures and other eastern religious writings are based on myths and legends. The pagan Greek and Roman religions were also based on myths.

Natural law—The God-built knowledge within each of us that there really is such a thing as right and wrong. Natural law includes cultural notions of justice, beauty, human dignity, ethics, love and truth. Because of human sin and rebellion against God, all cultural and personal understandings of natural law are clouded. To correct our clouded understanding, God gave us the Bible which contains the words of God and Jesus who *is* the Word of God.

Nature and mystery religions—Emphasize the earth, fertility and the spirits of the earth.

Neopaganism—The return to pre-Christian religions of the western world. Formerly, "pagan" was a term Christians used to apply to non-Christians. Today, pagan is a name that practitioners of old religions have taken for themselves.

New Age—Western reinterpretations of Hindu, Buddhist and occult mysticism rounded out with elements from Native American spirituality. The words "New Age" refer to the Aquarian age which occultists believe is dawning, bringing with it an era of enlightenment and peace. Encompassed within the New Age movement are various cults which emphasize mystic experiences.

Nirvana—Literally a "blowing out" or "cooling" of the fires of existence. In Buddhism it is the term used for the final release from the cycle of birth and death into bliss.

Occult, occultism—Literally meaning "hidden," it is a vague term used to cover a variety of groups or practices that involve contacting and using the knowledge and the power of the spirits of the dead and other spirits, including Satan and his demons.

Other sheep—People who are not in the fold of the good Shepherd, Jesus, whom He desires to bring in and save—the unsaved (see John 10:16).

Panentheism—The belief that all is *in* one, that there is a world or universal soul that is not separate from the world as we experience it and that we are all therefore connected to "the One."

Pantheism—The belief that God and the world are ultimately identical; all is God. Everything that exists constitutes a unity, and this all-inclusive unity is divine. God is equated with the forces and laws of the universe but is not a personal being.

Paradigm—An example or a model; a philosophical and theoretical framework within which theories and generalizations are formed.

Pluralism—A state of society in which members of diverse ethnic, racial, religious or social groups maintain an autonomous participation in and development of their traditional culture or special interest within the confines of a common civilization.

Psychological cults—such as Freudian and Jungian psychology eliminate God and substitute the individual's consciousness as the sole answer to his or her problems.

Quasi-Christian cults—Includes Jehovah's Witnesses, Mormons and others who radically depart from historic Christian faith, but try to convince potential converts that they are the true followers of Jesus.

Reaping—A metaphor for gathering the fruit or results of what one has planted. Also applies to character traits and the fruit of the Spirit. (See Galatians 6:7-9.)

Redemption—The act of being redeemed, that is being set free by paying a ransom. Christians are redeemed from eternal death to eternal life through God's gracious provision of Jesus' death on the cross (see Romans 3:23-25).

Reincarnation—The belief that the soul moves from one life and body to another. This movement is supposedly influenced by the actions a person has in his or her previous life. After many existences the soul is released from historical existence into the Absolute. This is a commonly held belief of religions affiliated with Hinduism.

Savior—Jesus, our Savior, was sent by God to save the world from sin.

Scientism—An exaggerated trust in the methods of natural science applied to all areas of investigation such as in philosophy, the social sciences and the humanities.

Scientology—Cult founded by science fiction writer L. Ron Hubbard. It is a mix of psychology, occultism and science fiction.

Self-determinism—Personal philosophy of life that a person alone totally determines his or her own life course.

Sowing—A metaphor used in the Bible that means the planting of thoughts, attitudes and beliefs that will grow and bring about consequences good or bad depending on what is sown (see Matthew 13:3-8,18-23; 2 Corinthians 9:6; Galatians 6:7-9).

Spiritual master—A guru or teacher in an eastern religion who claims supernatural ability and power.

Syncretism—The combination of two or more different forms of belief systems.

Taoism—A mystical Chinese religion founded by Lao-tzu (sixth century B.C.) that emphasizes freedom from desire, effortless action and simplicity. Taoism like Theravada Buddhism is more rigorist in its approach, emphasizing the cosmic and moral order of the universe.

Transcendentalism—A philosophy that asserts the primacy of the spiritual and the transcendental over the material and the empirical (idealism).

Transcendent and immanent—To say God is transcendent is to affirm that God is distinct from and over the physical universe; that God is free to act on and in the Creation according to the divine will. To say God is immanent is to affirm that God is everywhere present in the physical universe. Pantheists and panentheists believe "God" is immanent, but not transcendent, that "God" is part and parcel of the universe. However, Judaism and Christianity teach that God is both immanent and transcendent.

Transcendental meditation—A Hindu cult imported to the west by Maharishi Mahesh Yogi that focuses on a meditation technique in which a *mantra* (or short phrase or name of a god in the Sanskrit language) is chanted in order to foster calm, creativity and spiritual well-being.

Truth—In the New Testament truth refers to Christ, the salvation He brings and what He reveals about God. Jesus Christ is the way, the truth and the life (see John 14:6). A person is in the truth or knows the truth if his/her existence corresponds to what truth really is or should be. Many in our culture believe that truth is relative, that each of us creates our own truth and that "my truth" is not the same as "your truth."

Virgin—A woman who has not had sexual intercourse. Mary was a virgin when Jesus was born (see Matthew 1:18,22-24).

Watering—A metaphor used in the Bible to describe the nurturing and caring of those seeds of the gospel that are planted, or sown in a person's heart (see 1 Corinthians 3:6-8).

Wicca—A nature religion that seeks to be in harmony with and uses the powers of the spirits and timings of nature which, according to the Bible, is a form of witchcraft. Contemporary witches often prefer this Old English title for their practice of witchcraft.

Witness—The testimony of one who furnishes evidence or proof or has knowledge of an incident. Also a person giving testimony of Jesus rising from the dead (see Acts 1:8).

Witchcraft—The practice of magic or sorcery traditionally used by witches for evil ends. In the western world, witchcraft has evolved into neopaganism and ritual magic practices (see Galatians 5:19-21).

Yogi—A master of one or more methods of yoga (a Hindu system of meditation and self-control designed to produce spiritual insight) who teaches it to others.

Appendix C

Annotated Bibliography

Anderson, Neil T. and Elmer Towns. *Rivers of Revival.* Ventura, CA: Regal Books, 1998.

God is preparing His people for a great world harvest, but are we ready for revival? The authors share their startling insights into how God is now moving, seeking to pour Himself out on His people today—and what each of us must do to personally prepare for the challenge of reaching this world for Christ in our generation.

Barna, George. *Evangelism That Works.* Ventura, CA: Regal Books, 1995.

A look at the unsaved in the U. S.—who they are, what they want—and the evangelistic methods that are reaching them. Provides leaders with tangible, real-life tools for the task.

Behe, Michel J. *Darwin's Black Box.* New York City: Free Press, 1996.

Behe illuminates one of the most vexing problems in biology: how to account for the astonishing complexity that permeates all of life on this planet. He shows that the theory of evolution cannot adequately account for this complexity.

Bonnke, Reinhard. *Evangelism by Fire.* Sacramento, CA: Christ for All Nations, 1996.

This book will fire your faith and ignite a deep spiritual passion for the salvation of the lost.

Bryant, David. *Concerts of Prayer.* Ventura, CA: Regal Books, 1988.

Worldwide spiritual renewal is coming and prayer is leading the way. Learn how the tremendous power of group prayer can pave the way for the evangelization of your community, includes a small group study guide.

———. *Stand in the Gap.* Ventura, CA: Regal Books, 1997.

A revision of *In the Gap,* this excellent prayer and evangelism handbook shows Christians how they can get involved in what God is doing in the world. This book will reach men and women "where they live," giving them tips and suggestions on how to reach their friends, neighbors, city and nation for Christ.

Haggard, Ted and Jack Hayford. *Loving Your City into the Kingdom.* Ventura, CA: Regal Books, 1997.

Imagine your city astonishingly and wonderfully transformed by the power of God's love. Articles by 23 Christian leaders present proven ideas and strategies for bringing about a 21st century revival in your city.

Johnson, Philip E. *Darwin on Trial.* Downers Grove, IL: InterVarsity Press, 1993.
With a lawyer's skill, Johnson shows that the theory of evolution is based not on empirical data, but on faith in philosophical naturalism.

———. *Defeating Darwinism by Opening Minds.* Downers Grove, IL: InterVarsity Press, 1997.
This book is a great resource for high-school students, parents, teachers and youth pastors. It aims at defeating evolution by avoiding common mistakes in discussions about evolution, spotting deceptive arguments and grasping the basic scientific issues without getting bogged down in unnecessary details.

McDowell, Josh. *Evidence That Demands a Verdict, Volumes I and II.* Nashville, TN: Thomas Nelson Inc., 1993.
A compilation of arguments against the historic Christian faith and answers to these arguments from Scripture and scholars. Includes outstanding summaries of the evidence for the unique claims of Christ, the resurrection of Christ, and the reliability and authority of the Scriptures.

Ross, Hugh. *The Creator and the Cosmos: How the Greatest Scientific Discoveries of the Century Reveal God.* Colorado Springs: NavPress, 1993.
A readable, compelling journey through the most recent scientific findings, providing overwhelming support for the design of the universe.

Silvoso, Ed. *That None Should Perish.* Ventura, CA: Regal Books, 1994.
The definitive work on prayer evangelism teaches how to break through the barriers of unbelief and reach the people in your neighborhoods, cities and nations for Christ through the power of prayer.

Wagner, C. Peter. *Breaking Strongholds in Your City.* Ventura CA: Regal Books, 1993.
Learn how to identify the enemy's territory in your city, focus your prayers and take back your neighborhood for God.

Wagner, C. Peter. *Churches That Prayer.* Ventura CA: Regal Books, 1993.
Action prayer can change your church—and your life. Examine how prayer can help revitalize your congregation and break down the walls between your church and your community.

Wagner, C. Peter. *The New Apostolic Churches.* Ventura, CA: Regal Books, 1998.
The author explains the grassroots phenomenon in which God is raising up churches and leaders to help fulfill the last awesome push of the Great Commission.

Wagner, C. Peter. *Warfare Prayer*. Ventura, CA: Regal Books, 1992.
In the spiritual battle to reach the lost for Christ, you'll learn how to take up the weapon of prayer against the demonic realm, cautiously and wisely, as an informed and prepared warrior.

Video Resources

Barna, George. *10 Myths About Evangelism*. Ventura, CA: Gospel Light.
Help your church become truly evangelistic by asking a few simple questions.

Barna, George. *Trends That Are Changing Your Ministry World*. Gospel Light.
Discover how the world views religion, the Church and spiritual issues.

Barna, George. *What Evangelistic Churches Do*. Gospel Light.
Examine evangelistic efforts that are really working—and those that aren't.

Haggard, Ted. *Loving Your City into the Kingdom Video Seminar*. Gospel Light.
Witness an amazing outpouring of God's love on the people in your community. Ted Haggard shows you how, with practical steps you can take to reach your neighborhood for Christ and prepare your city to receive the blessings of God. Use this video seminar to mobilize your congregation and get ready for action! Includes a reproducible syllabus. (Approximately 200 minutes)

Silvoso, Ed. *That None Should Perish Video Seminar*. Ventura CA: Gospel Light.
Learn how the prayer life of your congregation can become a catalyst for reaching and taking cities and communities for God. This seminar instructs viewers in the fundamentals of prayer evangelism and shows them how the power of prayer in their church can effect change in the lives of millions. Includes a reproducible syllabus.

Prayer and Spiritual Warfare Video Seminar Series,

Hosted by C. Peter Wagner, each video contains two complete messages. Ventura, CA: Gospel Light.

Beckett, Bob. "Committing to Your Community." with
Silvoso, Ed. "Power to Reach Your City."
To break the enemy's grip on nonbelievers, we must go beyond our church and take God's love into the community around us. Discover how to uncover the potential that God has place in your community and how to redeem it in His name.

Jacobs, Cindy. "Releasing the Harvesters." with
Haggard, Ted. "Prayer Walking Your City."

Develop new passion for prayer! Discover how to maximize prayer opportunities and stimulate the Holy Spirit's activity to reach the lost and lead them to Christ.

Pierce, Chuck. "Releasing the Intercessory Mantle." with
Jackson, Larry. " Intercession for the Lost."

Become a more effective intercessor by identifying with sinners in your community, taking on their pain and suffering as if it were your own. Learn how to relate with sinners on such a deep level that God's awesome power and purpose will be set free to overcome the enemy and lead unbelievers to Christ.

Additional Resources

You now have the opportunity to keep updated on the best resources available for personal witnessing.

It is the author's prayer that there will be a great wave of personal witnessing efforts by Christians in North America. As part of the author's commitment to facilitate this, he has compiled and will maintain a current list of videos, books and other relevant tools that target the lost and the unchurched.

A copy of this list is available by sending a stamped self-addressed envelope to:

Douglas Shaw
P. O. Box 276384
Sacramento CA 95827
Phone: 916-362-8401
Fax: 916-362-3625

Any other correspondence pertaining to the ministry may also be mailed to the same address.